FLASHMAPS

NEW YORK

Editorial Updater
Martha Schulman

Cartographic Updater
Mapping Specialists

Proofreader
Susan Gryder

Editor
Robert Blake

Cover Design
Chie Ushio

Creative Director
Fabrizio La Rocca

Cartographer
David Lindroth

Designer
Tigist Getachew

Cartographic Contributors
Edward Faherty
Sheila Levin
Page Lindroth
Eric Rudolph

www.fodors.com

Fodor's Travel Publications
New York, Toronto, London, Sydney, Auckland

Contents

Special Sales

Fodor's Travel Publications are available at special discounts for bulk purchases for sales promotions or premiums. Special editions, including personalized covers, excerpts of existing guides, and corporate imprints, can be created in large quantities for special needs. For more information, contact your local bookseller or write to Special Markets/ Premium Sales, 1745 Broadway, MD 6-2, New York, NY 10019, or e-mail specialmarkets@randomhouse.com.

ISBN 1-4000-1510-3   **ISSN 1527-4853**

PRINTED IN CHINA 10 9 8 7 6 5 4 3

Area Codes: Manhattan (212, 646, 917); Bronx, Brooklyn, Queens, Staten Island (718, 347); Nassau/Suffolk (516); Northern NJ (201, 973). All (212) unless otherwise noted.

EMERGENCIES

AAA Emergency Road Service
☎ 800/222-4357

Ambulance, Fire, Police ☎ 911

Animal Bites ☎ 676-2483

Animal Medical Center
☎ 838-8100

Arson Hotline ☎ 800/FIRE-TIP

Child Abuse ☎ 800/342-3720

Crime Victim Hotline ☎ 577-7777

Domestic Violence Hotline
☎ 800/621-HOPE

Drug Abuse ☎ 800/395-3400

Lesbian and Gay Anti-Violence Project ☎ 714-1184

Mental Health Crisis Hotline/LifeNet
☎ 800/543-3638

Poison Control ☎ 340-4494

Rape Hotline ☎ 800/656-4673

Runaway Hotline
☎ 800/621-4000

Sexual Assualt Reports
☎ 267-7273

Suicide Prevention/Samaritans
☎ 673-3000

SERVICES

AAA ☎ 757-2000
www.aaa.com

ACLU/NY ☎ 344-3005
www.aclu.org

AIDS Hotline (CDC)
☎ 800/342-2437
www.cdc.gov

AIDS Hotline (NY)
☎ 800/541-AIDS

Alcoholics Anonymous
☎ 647-1680
www.aa.org

Amex Lost Travelers Checks
☎ 800/221-7282

ASPCA ☎ 876-7700

Better Business Bureau
☎ 533-6200
www.newyork.bbb.org

Big Apple Greeters ☎ 669-2896
www.bigapplegreeters.org

Convention & Visitor's Bureau
☎ 484-1200; 800/692-8474
www.nycvisit.com

Dept of Aging ☎ 442-1000

Dept of Consumer Affairs
☎ 487-4444

Dept of Motor Vehicles
☎ 645-5550
www.nydmv.state.ny.us

Housing Authority ☎ 306-3000

HRA Infoline ☎ 877/472-8411

Immigration Information Line
☎ 800/375-528
www.uscis.gov

Legal Aid Society ☎ 577-3300

Lesbian & Gay Community Service Center ☎ 620-7310
www.gaycenter.org

Mayor's Office for People With Disabilities ☎ 788-2830

Medicare ☎ 800/MED-ICAR
www.medicare.gov

NY City Information ☎ 311
www.nyc.gov

NY Public Library Telephone Reference Service ☎ 340-0849
www.nypl.org

Overeaters Anonymous
☎ 206-8621
www.overeatersanonymous.org

Passport Information
☎ 206-3500

Planned Parenthood ☎ 274-7200
www.ppfa.org

Social Security ☎ 800/772-1213

Taxi Complaints ☎ 302-8294

Towaways ☎ 869-2929

Traveler's Aid ☎ 718/656-4870

24-Hour Locksmith ☎ 247-6747

UN Information ☎ 963-1234
www.un.org

US Customs ☎ 800/697-3662
www.customs.ustreas.gov

US Post Office ☎ 800/ASK-USPS
www.usps.com

WALKING TOURS

Adventure on a Shoestring
☎ 265-2663

Big Onion Walking Tours
☎ 439-1090
www.bigonion.com

Central Park Bike Tours
☎ 541-8759

Dr. Phil's NY Talks and Walks
☎ 888/377-4455
www.newyorktalksandwalks.com

Joyce Gold History Tours ☎ 242-5762
www.nyctours.com

Municipal Art Society ☎ 935-3960
www.mas.org

NYC Cultural Walking Tours
☎ 979-2388

NYC Discovery Walking Tours
☎ 465-3331

Radical Walking Tours
☎ 718/492-0069

SITE TOURS

Central Park ☎ 360-2726
www.centralpark.org

Governor's Island
☎ 480-5732; 514-8296
www.govisland.com

Lincoln Center ☎ 875-5350
www.lincolncenter.org

Madison Square Garden
☎ 465-6080
www.thegarden.com

Radio City ☎ 247-4777
www.radiocity.com

Rockefeller Center Tour ☎ 664-3700
www.rockefellercentertour.com

UN Tours ☎ 963-8687
www.un.org

Yankee Stadium Tours
☎ 718/579-4531
www.yankees.com

BUS TOURS

Gray Line ☎ 800/669-0051

Harlem Spirituals ☎ 391-0900
www.harlemspirituals.com

New York Sightseeing
☎ 445-0848
www.newyorksightseeing.com

BOAT TOURS

Circle Line/Seaport Liberty Cruises
☎ 563-3200
www.circlelineferry.com

NY Waterway ☎ 800/53-FERRY

Spirit Cruises of NY
☎ 866/399-8439
www.spiritcruises.com

World Yacht Cruises ☎ 630-8100
www.worldyacht.com

HELICOPTER TOURS

Helicopter Flight Services
☎ 355-0801
www.heliny.com

NY Helicopter Tours ☎ 361-6060
www.newyorkhelicopter.com

PARKS AND RECREATION

Bronx Zoo ☎ 718/367-1010
www.bronxzoo.com

Brooklyn Botanic Garden
☎ 718/623-7200
www.bbg.org

Central Park Boat Rental
☎ 517-2233

Central Park Conservancy
☎ 310-6600
www.centralpark.org

Central Park Tennis Center
☎ 360-8133

Central Park Zoo ☎ 861-6030
www.centralpark.org

Downtown Boathouse
☎ 646/613-0375

Empire Skate Club ☎ 774-1774
www.empireskate.org

Five Borough Bicycle Club
☎ 932-2300
www.5bbc.org

Governor's Island
☎ 480-5732; 514-8296
www.govisland.com

Hudson River Park ☎ 533-PARK
www.hudsonriver.org

National Parks of NY Harbor
☎ 718/354-4551 www.nps.gov

NY Botanic Garden
☎ 718/817-8700
www.nybg.org

NY Cycle Club ☎ 828-5711
www.nycc.org

NY Horticultural Society
☎ 757-0915
www.hsny.org

NY Road Runners ☎ 860-2280
www.nyrrc.org

Parks Events ☎ 888/NY-PARKS
www.nycgovparks.org

Prospect Park ☎ 718/965-8989
www.prospectpark.org

**Riverside Park 96th St Tennis
Center** ☎ 978-0277

Shorewalkers ☎ 663-2167
www.shorewalkers.org

Transportation Alternatives
☎ 629-8080
www.transalt.org

SPECTATOR SPORTS

Aqueduct & Belmont Race Tracks
☎ 718/641-4700
www.nyra.com

Brooklyn Cyclones
☎ 718/449-8497
www.brooklyncyclones.com

Continental Arena
☎ 201/935-3900
www.meadowlands.com

Madison Square Garden
☎ 465-6741
www.thegarden.com

Meadowlands Box Office
☎ 201/935-3900
www.meadowlands.com

Meadowlands Race Track
☎ 201/935-8500

Nassau Coliseum ☎ 516/794-9300
www.nassaucoliseum.com

NJ Devils ☎ 201/935-6050
www.newjerseydevils.com

NJ Nets ☎ 800/7NJ-NETS
www.nba.com/nets

NY Giants ☎ 201/935-8111
www.giants.com

NY Islanders ☎ 516/501-6700
www.newyorkislanders.com

NY Jets ☎ 516/560-8200
www.newyorkjets.com

NY Knicks ☎ 465-5867
www.nyknicks.com

NY Liberty ☎ 877/WNBA-TIX
www.nyliberty.com

NY Mets ☎ 718/507-8499
www.mets.com

NY Rangers ☎ 465-6000
www.newyorkrangers.com

NY Yankees ☎ 718/293-6000
www.yankees.com

Shea Stadium ☎ 718/507-6387

Staten Island Yankees
☎ 718/720-9265
www.si.yanks.com

US Open Tennis ☎ 718/760-6387
www.usopen.org

Yonkers Raceway
☎ 914/968-4200
www.yonkersraceway.com

TRANSPORTATION

Access-a-Ride ☎ 877/337-2017

Airport Travel Info
☎ 800/AIR-RIDE

Airtrain JFK ☎ 877/535-2478

Airtrain Newark ☎ 888/397-4636
www.panynj.gov/airtrainnewark

Amtrak ☎ 800/872-7245
www.amtrak.com

Bus & Subway Accessibility
☎ 718/596-8585

Bus & Subway Customer Service
☎ 718/330-3322

Bus & Subway Information
☎ 718/330-1234

Bus & Subway Service Status
☎ 718/243-7777
www.mta.nyc.ny.us

Coach-USA ☎ 877/894-9155

Ellis Island/Statue of Liberty Ferry
☎ 269-5755
www.circlelineferry.com

EZ Pass Information
☎ 800/333-8655
www.e-zpassny.com

Fire Island Ferries
☎ 631/665-3600

Greyhound Bus Lines
☎ 800/231-2222
www.greyhound.com

JFK Airport ☎ 718/244-4444
www.panynj.gov

La Guardia Airport
☎ 718/533-3400
www.panynj.gov

Long Island Railroad (LIRR)
☎ 718/217-5477
www.mta.nyc.ny.us

Martz Trailways
☎ 800/233-8604
www.martztrailways.com

Metro-North ☎ 532-4900;
800/METRO-INFO
www.mta.nyc.ny.us

NJ Transit ☎ 973/762-5100
www.njtransit.com

NY Airport Service
☎ 718/875-8200

NY Waterway Ferries
☎ 800/53-FERRY
www.nywaterway.com

Newark Airport ☎ 973/961-6000
www.panynj.gov

Olympia Airport Express
☎ 877/894-9155

Passenger Ship Terminal
☎ 246-5451

PATH ☎ 800/234-7284
www.panynj.gov/path

Peter Pan Bonanza
☎ 888/751-8000
www.bonanzabus.com

Peter Pan Trailways
☎ 800/343-9999
www.peterpanbus.com

Port Authority Bus Information
☎ 564-8484

Roosevelt Island Tram
☎ 832-4543
www.rioc.com/transportation.html

SeaStreak Ferry ☎ 800/262-8743
www.seastreak.com

Short Line ☎ 800/631-2628
www.shortlinebus.com

Staten Island Ferry
☎ 718/815-2628
www.siferry.com

SuperShuttle ☎ BLUE-VAN
www.supershuttle.com

Trailways ☎ 800/858-8555
www.trailways.com

Triborough Bridge and Tunnel Authority ☎ 360-3000
www.mta.nyc.ny.us/bandt

Vermont Transit ☎ 800/451-3292
www.vermonttransit.com

Water Taxi ☎ 742-1969
www.nywatertaxi.com

ENTERTAINMENT

Big Apple Circus ☎ 268-2500

Broadway Line ☎ 302-4111

Brooklyn Academy of Music
☎ 718/636-4100
www.bam.org

Carnegie Hall ☎ 247-7800
www.carnegiehall.org

Central Park Summerstage
☎ 360-2777
www.summerstage.org

City Center City Tix ☎ 581-1212
www.citycenter.org

Guggenheim Museum
☎ 423-3500
www.guggenheim.org

Historic House Museums
☎ 360-8282

Jazz Line ☎ 479-7888

Lincoln Center ☎ 546-2656
www.lincolncenter.org

Metropolitan Museum
☎ 535-7710
www.metmuseum.org

Movie Phone ☎ 777-FILM

Museum of Modern Art
☎ 708-9400
www.moma.org

NYC On Stage ☎ 768-1818
www.tdf.org

Radio City Music Hall ☎ 247-4777
www.radiocity.com

**Reduced Price Theatre Tickets
(TKTS)** ☎ 768-1818
www.tdf.org

**Shakespeare in the Park/Delacorte
Theater** ☎ 861-7283
www.publictheater.org

Telecharge ☎ 239-6200

Ticket Central ☎ 279-4200

Ticketmaster ☎ 307-7171

Whitney Museum ☎ 570-3676
www.whitney.org

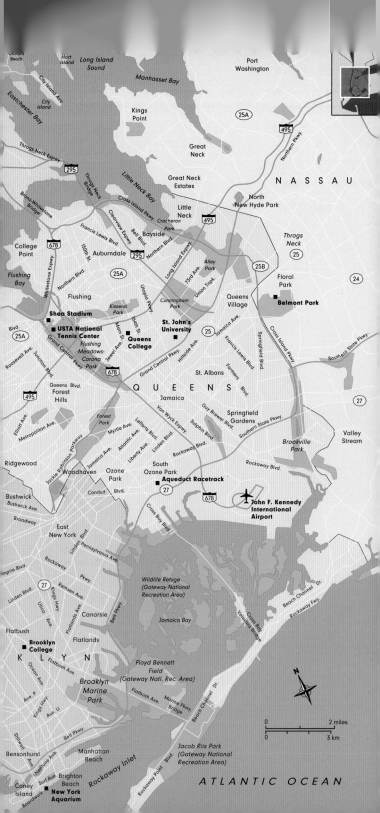

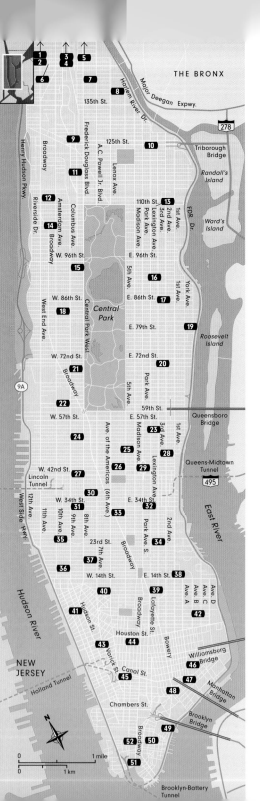

Listed Alphabetically

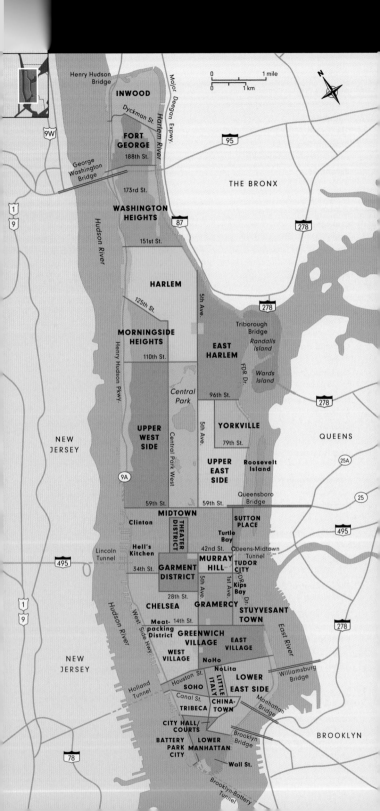

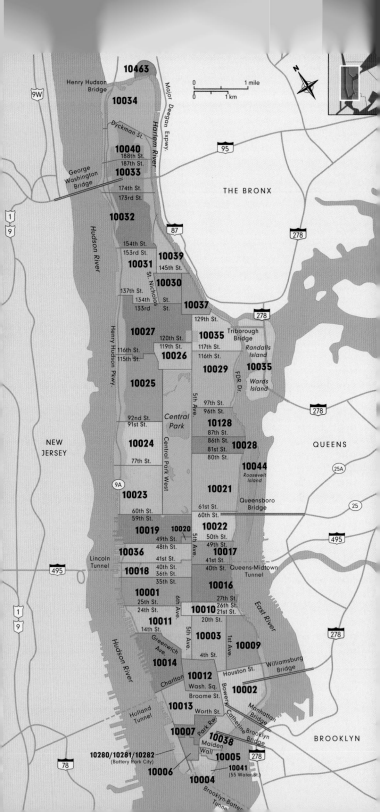

Streets	West End Ave.	Broadway	Amsterdam Ave.	Columbus Ave.	Central Park West
94-96	700-737	2520-2554	702-733	701-740	350-360
92-94	660-699	2476-2519	656-701	661-700	322-336
90-92	620-659	2440-2475	620-655	621-660	300-320
88-90	578-619	2401-2439	580-619	581-620	279-295
86-88	540-577	2361-2400	540-579	541-580	262-275
84-86	500-539	2321-2360	500-539	501-540	241-257
82-84	460-499	2281-2320	460-499	461-500	212-239
80-82	420-459	2241-2280	420-459	421-460	211
78-80	380-419	2201-2240	380-419	381-420	American Museum of Natural History
76-78	340-379	2161-2200	340-379	341-380	
74-76	300-339	2121-2160	300-339	301-340	145-160
72-74	262-299	2081-2114	261-299	261-300	121-135
70-72	221-261	2040-2079	221-260	221-260	101-115
68-70	176-220	1999-2030	181-220	181-220	80-99
66-68	122-175	1961-1998	140-180	141-180	65-79
64-66	74-121	1920-1960	100-139	101-140	50-55
62-64	44-73	Lincoln Center	60-99	61-100	25-33
60-62	20-43	1841-1880	20-59	21-60	15
58-60	2-19	Columbus Circle	1-19	2-20	Columbus Circle

	11th Ave.	Broadway	10th Ave.	9th Ave.	8th Ave.	7th Ave.	6th Ave.
56-58	823-854	1752-1791	852-889	864-907	946-992	888-921	1381-1419
54-56	775-822	1710-1751	812-851	824-863	908-945	842-887	1341-1377
52-54	741-774	1674-1709	772-811	782-823	870-907	798-841	1301-1330
50-52	701-740	1634-1673	737-770	742-781	830-869	761-797	1261-1297
48-50	665-700	1596-1633	686-735	702-741	791-829	720-760	1221-1260
46-48	625-664	1551-1595	654-685	662-701	735-790	701-719	1180-1217
44-46	589-624	1514-1550	614-653	622-661	701-734	Times Square	1141-1178
42-44	553-588	1472-1513	576-613	582-621	661-700		1100-1140
40-42	503-552	1440-1471	538-575	Port Authority	620-660	560-598	1061-1097
38-40	480-502	1400-1439	502-537		570-619	522-559	1020-1060
36-38	431-471	1352-1399	466-501	468-501	520-569	482-521	981-1019
34-36	405-430	Macy's	430-465	432-467	480-519	442-481	Herald Square
32-34	360-404	1260-1282	380-429	412-431	442-479	Penn Station	
30-32	319-359	1220-1279	341-379	Post Office	403-441	362-399	855-892
28-30	282-318	1178-1219	314-340	314-351	362-402	322-361	815-844
26-28	242-281	1135-1177	288-313	262-313	321-361	282-321	775-814
24-26	202-241	1100-1134	239-287	230-261	281-320	244-281	733-774
22-24	162-201	940-1099	210-238	198-229	236-280	210-243	696-732
20-22	120-161	902-939	162-209	167-197	198-235	170-209	656-695
18-20	82-119	873-901	130-161	128-166	162-197	134-169	613-655
16-18	54-81	860-872	92-129	92-127	126-161	100-133	574-612
14-16	26-53	Union Square	58-91	44-91	80-125	64-99	530-573

Crosstown Street Address Finder

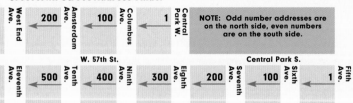

West End Ave. ← 200 Amsterdam Ave. ← 100 Columbus Ave. ← 1 Central Park W.

NOTE: Odd number addresses are on the north side, even numbers are on the south side.

W. 57th St.

Eleventh Ave. ← 500 Tenth Ave. ← 400 Ninth Ave. ← 300 Eighth Ave. ← 200 Seventh Ave. ← 100 Sixth Ave. ← 1 Fifth Ave.

Central Park S.

5th Ave.	Madison Ave.	Park Ave.	Lexington Ave.	3rd Ave.	2nd Ave.	1st Ave.	Streets
1130–1148	1340–1379	1199–1236	1449–1486	1678–1709	1817–1868	1817–1855	94–96
1109–1125	1295–1335	1160–1192	1400–1444	1644–1677	1766–1808	1780–1811	92–94
1090–1107	1254–1294	1120–1155	1361–1396	1601–1643	1736–1763	1740–1779	90–92
1070–1089	1220–1250	1080–1114	1311–1355	1568–1602	1700–1739	1701–1735	88–90
1050–1069	1178–1221	1044–1076	1280–1301	1530–1566	1660–1698	1652–1689	86–88
1030–1048	1130–1171	1000–1035	1248–1278	1490–1529	1624–1659	1618–1651	84–86
1010–1028	1090–1128	960–993	1210–1248	1450–1489	1584–1623	1578–1617	82–84
990–1009	1058–1088	916–959	1164–1209	1410–1449	1538–1583	1540–1577	80–82
970–989	1012–1046	878–911	1120–1161	1374–1409	1498–1537	1495–1539	78–80
950–969	974–1006	840–877	1080–1116	1330–1373	1456–1497	1462–1494	76–78
930–947	940–970	799–830	1036–1071	1290–1329	1420–1454	1429–1460	74–76
910–929	896–939	760–791	1004–1032	1250–1289	1389–1417	1344–1384	72–74
895–907	856–872	720–755	962–993	1210–1249	1328–1363	1306–1343	70–72
870–885	813–850	680–715	926–961	1166–1208	1296–1327	1266–1300	68–70
850–860	772–811	640–679	900–922	1130–1165	1260–1295	1222–1260	66–68
830–849	733–771	600–639	841–886	1084–1129	1222–1259	1168–1221	64–66
810–828	690–727	560–599	803–842	1050–1083	1180–1221	1130–1167	62–64
790–807	654–680	520–559	770–802	1010–1049	1140–1197	1102–1129	60–62
755–789	621–649	476–519	722–759	972–1009	Queensborough Bridge		58–60
720–754	572–611	434–475	677–721	942–968	1066–1101	1026–1063	56–58
680–719	532–568	408–430	636–665	894–933	1028–1062	985–1021	54–56
656–679	500–531	360–399	596–629	856–893	984–1027	945–984	52–54
626–655	452–488	320–350	556–593	818–855	944–983	889–944	50–52
600–625	412–444	280–300	518–555	776–817	902–943	860–888	48–50
562–599	377–400	240–277	476–515	741–775	862–891	827	46–48
530–561	346–375	Met Life (200)	441–475	702–735	824–860	785	United Nations	44–46
500–529	316–345	Grand Central	395–435	660–701	793–823		42–44
460–499	284–315		354–394	622–659	746–773	Tudor City	40–42
424–459	250–283	68–99	314–353	578–621	707–747	666–701	38–40
392–423	218–249	40–67	284–311	542–577	666–700	Midtown Tunnel	36–38
352–391	188–217	5–35	240–283	508–541	622–659	599–626	34–36
320–351	152–184	1–4	196–239	470–507	585–621	556–598	32–34
284–319	118–150	444–470 Park Ave.	160–195	432–469	543–581	Kips Bay	30–32
250–283	79–117	404–431 Park Ave. S.	120–159	394–431	500–541	NYU Hosp.	28–30
213–249	50–78	364–403	81–119	358–393	462–499	446–478	26–28
201–212	11–37	323–361	40–77	321–355	422–461	411–445	24–26
172–200	1–7	286–322	9–39	282–318	382–421	390–410	22–24
154–170		251–285	1–8	244–281	344–381	315–389	20–22
109–153		221–250	70–78	206–243	310–343	310–314	18–20
85–127		184–220	40–69	166–205	301–309	280–309	16–18
69–108		Union Square	2–30	126–165	230–240	240–279	14–16

Lexington Ave. / Irving Pl. (column label)

Fifth Ave.   Madison Ave.   Park Ave.   Lexington Ave.   Third Ave.   Second Ave.   First Ave.

1 → 100 → 140 → 200 → 300 → 400 →

MAP 6
Streetfinder/The Village & Downtown

Union Sq. Park

A   B   C

W. 15th St.

M A,C,E,L   **M** 1,2,3,9   **M** F,L,V   W. 14th St.   **M** L,N,Q,R,W, 4,5,6

Seventh Ave. S.   W. 13th St.
Greenwich Ave.   W. 12th St.   Fifth Ave.
Little W. 12th St.   Eighth Ave.   W. 11th St.   University Pl.
Gansevoort St.   W. 4th St.   Avenue of the Americas   W. 10th St.
Horatio St.   Waverly Pl.   W. 9th St.
Jane St.   Abingdon Square   W. 8th St.   **N,R,W**
W. 12th St.   Milligan Pl.   Greene St.   MacDougal St.   **M**
Bethune St.   Patchin Pl.   Gay St.   MacDougal Alley   Washington Mews

Bank St.   Perry St.   Sheridan Square   Waverly Pl.   Washington Sq. N.   Waverly Pl.
Charles St.   W. 10th St.   **M**   W. Washington Pl.   Washington Square Park   E. Washington Pl.
W. 11th St.   Christopher St.   1,9   **M** A,B,C,D, E,F,V   Washington Sq. S.   **New York University**   W. 3rd St.
Greenwich St.   Grove St.   Jones St.   Cornelia St.   Bleecker St.   Minetta La.   Bleecker St.
Washington St.   Barrow St.   Bedford St.   Father Demo Sq.
Morton St.   Commerce St.   Carmine St.   Ave. of the Americas   MacDougal St.   W. Houston St.   **M**
Leroy St.   St. Luke's Pl.   Downing St.   Sullivan St.   Thompson St.   **B,D,F,V**
Clarkson St.   1,9   Spring St.   **C,E**   West Broadway   **N,R**
Hudson River Park   W. Houston St.   Varick St.   Dominick St.   **M**
King St.   Charlton St.   (Sixth Ave.)   Wooster St.   Mercer St.   Broadway
Hudson St.   Vandam St.   Spring St.   Grand St.
Washington St.   Broome St.   Holland Tunnel Entrance   1,9   **M** A,C,E   Canal St.   **N,Q,**
Watts St.   Holland Tunnel Exit   Church St.   Lispenard St.   **M**   Greene St.   Broadway
Desbrosses St.   Greenwich St.   Hudson St.   Varick St.   Walker St.   White St.   **M** 1,9   Franklin St.
Vestry St.   Laight St.   Ericsson Pl.   Leonard St.   Worth St.   Catherine La.
Hubert St.   Beach St.   N. Moore St.   Franklin St.   West Broadway   Thomas St.   Federal Plaza
Manhattan Community College   Harrison St.   Jay St.   Staple St.   Duane St.   Reade St.
Independence Plaza   1,2,3,9   **M** A,C
Chambers St.   Chambers St.

Hudson River

Holland Tunnel

Warren St.   Warren St.   **M** R,W
Terrace   Park Pl. W   Murray St.   City Hall Park   **M** 2,3
Murray St.   Park Pl.   **M** R,W
North End Ave.   Washington St.   Barclay St.   **M** C,E
Vesey St.   Vesey St.   Fulton St.   **M** A,C
World Financial Center   **World Trade Center Site**   1,9 (Closed)   **M** 4,5   **M** 4,5
Dey St.   **M** 4,5
Liberty St.   Cortlandt St.   **M** N,R
Albany St.   Liberty St.   Cedar St.
Carlisle St.   Thames   Pine St.
Albany St.   Trinity Pl.   Rector St.   **M** 4,5 Wall St
BATTERY PARK CITY   West Thames St.   1,9   **M** R,W Exchange Pl.   New St.
Battery Pl.   Morris St.   Whitehall St.   Broadway
3rd Pl.   Battery Place   Little West St.   Bowling Green
2nd Pl.   Bridge St.
1st Pl.   Battery Pl.   **M** 4,5   State St.

N

0   1200 feet
0   400 meters

Robert F. Wagner Jr. Park

A   B   C   Battery Park

MAP **6** Streetfinder/The Village & Downtown

Letter codes refer to grid sectors on preceding map

Abingdon Sq. B1
Albany St. B6, C5
Allen St. D2, D3
Ann St. C5, D5
Astor Pl. D1
Attorney St. E2
Ave. A E1, E2
Ave. B E1, E2
Ave. C E1, E2
Ave. D E1, E2
Ave. of the Americas (Sixth Ave.) C1, C4
Bank St. A2, B1
Barclay St. C5
Barrow St. B2
Baruch Pl. F2
Battery Pl. C6
Baxter St. D3, D4
Bayard St. D4
Beach St. B4
Beaver St. C6, D6
Bedford St. B2, C2
Beekman St. D5
Bethune St. A1, B1
Bleecker St. B1, D2
Bond St. D2
Bowery D2, D4
Bowling Green C6
Bridge St. C6, D6
Broadway C1, C6
Brooklyn Battery Tunnel C6, D6
Brooklyn Bridge D5, F5
Broome St. B3, E3
Burling Slip D5
Canal St. C3, E3
Cardinal Hayes Plaza D4
Carlisle St. C6
Carmine St. B2
Catherine La. C4
Catherine Slip E4
Catherine St. D4, E4
Cedar St. C5, D5
Central Market D3
Centre St. D3, D5
Chambers St. B4, D4
Charles St. B1, B2

Charlton St. B3, C3
Chatham Sq. D4
Cherry St. E4, F3
Christopher St. B2, C1
Chrystie St. D2, D3
Church St. C4, C5
Clarkson St. B2, B3
Cleveland Pl. D3
Clinton St. E2, E4
Coenties Slip D6
Columbia St. E2, E3
Commerce St. B2
Cooper Sq. D1, D2
Cornelia St. B2
Cortlandt St. C5
Crosby St. C2, C3
Delancey St. D3, E3
Depyster St. D6
Desbrosses St. B3
Dey St. C5
Division St. D4, E4
Dominick St. B3, C3
Dover St. D5
Downing St. B2, C2
Doyers St. D4
Duane St. C4, D4
East Broadway D4, E3
East Houston St. D2, F2
East River Drive F1, F3
East Washington Pl. C2
Eighth Ave. B1
Eldridge St. D2, D3
Elizabeth St. D2, D4
Elk St. D4
Ericsson Pl. C4
Essex St. E2, E3
Exchange Pl. C6, D6
Father Demo Sq. C2
FDR Dr. F1, F3
Federal Plaza C4, D4
Fifth Ave. C1
First Ave. D1, D2
Fletcher St. D5
Foley Sq. D4
Forsyth St. D4, E4
Fourth Ave. D1
Franklin St. C4

Front St. D6
Fulton St. C5, D5
Gansevoort St. A1, B1
Gay St. B1, C1
Gold St. D5
Gouverneur La. D6
Gouverneur St. E3
Grand St. C3, F3
Great Jones St. D2
Greene St. C1, C3
Greenwich Ave. B1, C1
Greenwich St. B1, C6
Grove St. B2
Hanover Sq. D6
Hanover St. D6
Harrison St. B4, C4
Henry St. D4, E3
Hester St. D3, E3
Hogan Pl. D4
Holland Tunnel A4, C3
Horatio St. A1, B1
Hubert St. B4
Hudson St. B1, C4
Independence Plaza B4, C4
Jackson St. F3
James St. D4
Jane St. A1, B1
Jay St. C4
Jefferson St. E3
John St. C5, D5
Jones Alley D2
Jones St. B2
Kenmare St. D3
Kent Pl. D4
King St. B3, C3
Lafayette St. D1, D4
LaGuardia Pl. C2
Laight St. B4
Leonard St. C4
Leroy St. B2
Lewis St. F3
Liberty St. C5
Lispenard St. C4
Little W. 12th St. A1
Ludlow St. E2, E3
MacDougal Alley C1
MacDougal St. C1, C3

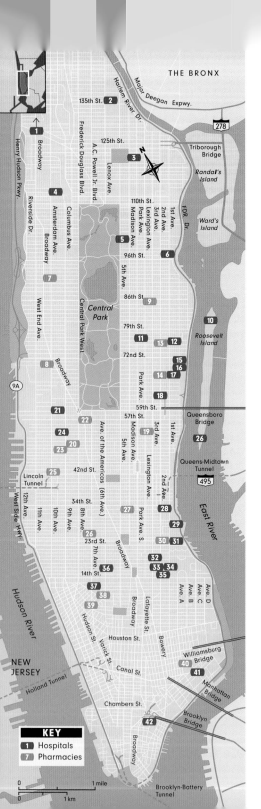

THE BRONX

135th St.

Harlem River Dr.

Major Deegan Expwy.

278

Triborough Bridge

Randall's Island

Ward's Island

Broadway

Henry Hudson Pkwy.

Riverside Dr.

Frederick Douglass Blvd.

A.C. Powell Jr. Blvd.

125th St.

Lenox Ave.

110th St.

Madison Ave.

Park Ave.

Lexington Ave.

2nd Ave.

3rd Ave.

1st Ave.

FDR. Dr.

Columbus Ave.

Amsterdam Ave.

Broadway

West End Ave.

96th St.

5th Ave.

86th St

Central Park

79th St.

Roosevelt Island

72nd St.

Central Park West

Park Ave.

9A

Broadway

57th St.

Queensboro Bridge

Queens-Midtown Tunnel

495

Ave. of the Americas (6th Ave.)

Madison Ave.

5th Ave.

3rd Ave.

1st Ave.

2nd Ave.

42nd St.

Lincoln Tunnel

34th St.

12th Ave.

West Side Hwy.

11th Ave.

10th Ave.

9th Ave.

8th Ave.

7th Ave.

Lexington Ave.

Park Ave. S

East River

23rd St.

Broadway

14th St.

Ave. D

Ave. C

Ave. B

Ave. A

Lafayette St.

Bowery

Hudson River

NEW JERSEY

Houston St.

Hudson St.

Varick St.

Canal St.

Williamsburg Bridge

Manhattan Bridge

Holland Tunnel

Chambers St.

Broadway

Brooklyn Bridge

KEY

1 Hospitals

7 Pharmacies

0 — 1 mile
0 — 1 km

Brooklyn-Battery Tunnel

Listed Alphabetically

HOSPITALS

Bellevue Hospital Center, 29.
462 First Ave ☎ 562-4141

Beth Israel Med Center, 34.
First Ave at 16th St ☎ 420-2000

Cabrini Med Center, 32. 227 E 19th St
☎ 995-6000

Coler-Goldwater Memorial, 10.
900 Main St, Roosevelt Island
☎ 848-6000

Coler-Goldwater Memorial, 26.
1 Main St, Roosevelt Island
☎ 318-8000

Gouverneur, 41. 227 Madison St
☎ 318-8000

Gracie Square (Psychiatric), 12.
420 E 76th St ☎ 988-4400

Harlem Hospital Center, 2.
506 Lenox Ave ☎ 939-1000

Joint Diseases, 33. 301 E 17th St
☎ 598-6000

Lenox Hill, 11. 100 E 77th St
☎ 434-2000

Manhattan Eye, Ear, & Throat, 18.
210 E 64th St ☎ 838-9200

Memorial Sloan-Kettering (Cancer), 17. 1275 York Ave ☎ 639-2000

Metropolitan, 6. 1901 First Ave
☎ 423-6262

Mount Sinai, 5. Fifth Ave at 100th St
☎ 241-6500

New York Eye & Ear, 35. 310 E 14th St
☎ 979-4000

New York Foundling (Children), 36.
590 Sixth Ave ☎ 633-9300

North General, 3.
Madison Ave at 122nd St ☎ 423-4000

NY Harbor/VA Hospital, 31.
408 First Ave ☎ 686-7500

NYU Downtown, 42.
170 William St ☎ 312-5000

NY Presbyterian Columbia Med Ctr, 1.
622 W 168th St ☎ 305-2500

NY Presbyterian Cornell-Weill Med Center, 16.
525 E 68th St ☎ 746-5454

NYU Med Center, 28. 550 First Ave
☎ 263-7300

Payne Whitney (Psychiatric), 16.
525 E 68th St ☎ 746-0331

Special Surgery, 15. 535 E 70th St
☎ 606-1000

St Luke's–Roosevelt, 4.
1111 Amsterdam Ave
☎ 523-4000

St Luke's–Roosevelt, 21.
428 W 59th St ☎ 523-4000

St Vincent's Midtown, 24.
415 W 51st St ☎ 586-1500

St Vincent's, 37. 153 W 11th St
☎ 604-7000

LATE-NIGHT/24-HOUR PHARMACIES

Apthorp Pharmacy, 8.
2201 Broadway ☎ 800/775-3582

Bigelow Pharmacy, 38.
414 Sixth Ave ☎ 533-2700

CVS Pharmacy, 19.
630 Lexington Ave ☎ 917/369-8688
(24-hour)

CVS Pharmacy, 25. 500 W 42nd St
☎ 244-4285

CVS Pharmacy, 30. 342 E 23rd St
☎ 505-1555 (24-hour)

Duane Reade, 7. 2465 Broadway
☎ 799-3172 (24-hour)

Duane Reade, 13. 1279 Third Ave
☎ 744-2668 (24-hour)

Duane Reade, 22. 224 W 57th St
☎ 541-9708 (24-hour)

Duane Reade, 23.
721 Ninth Ave ☎ 246-0168

Eckerd Drug, 14. 1299 Second Ave
☎ 772-0104

Rite Aid, 9. 146 E 86th St
☎ 876-0600 (24-hour)

Rite Aid, 20. 303 W 50th St
☎ 247-8384 (24-hour)

Rite Aid, 40. 408 Grand St
☎ 529-7115 (24-hour)

Village Apothecary, 39.
346 Bleecker St ☎ 807-7566

Walgreens, 27.
350 Fifth Ave ☎ 868-5659 (24-hour)

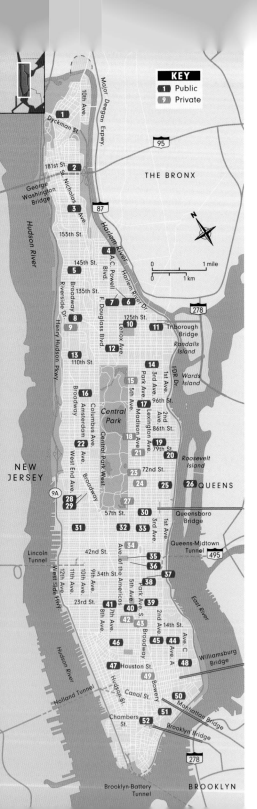

Listed Alphabetically

CONSULATES

Argentina, 23. 12 W 56th St
☎ 603-0400

Australia, 24. 150 E 42nd St
☎ 351-6500

Austria, 11. 31 E 69th St ☎ 737-6400

Bahamas, 59. 231 E 46th St
☎ 421-6420

Bahrain, 60. 866 Second Ave.
☎ 223-6200

Bangladesh, 71. 211 E 43rd St
☎ 599-6767

Barbados, 69. 800 Second Ave
☎ 867-8435

Belarus, 72. 708 third Ave
☎ 682-5392

Belgium, 25. 1330 Sixth Ave
☎ 586-5110

Bhutan, 64. 763 First Ave ☎ 682-2268

Bolivia, 71. 211 E 43rd St ☎ 687-0530

Brazil, 55. 747 Third Ave
☎ 832-6868

Bulgaria, 18. 121 E 62nd St
☎ 935-4646

Canada, 51. 1251 Sixth Ave
☎ 596-1628

Chile, 36. 866 UN Plaza ☎ 980-3366

China, 54. 520 Twelfth Ave
☎ 244-9456

Colombia, 22. 140 E 57th St
☎ 355-7776

Costa Rica, 100. 80 Wall St
☎ 425-2620

Croatia, 89. 369 Lexington Ave
☎ 599-3066

Cyprus, 94. 13 E 40th St ☎ 686-6016

Czech Republic, 2.
1109 Madison Ave ☎ 717-5643

Denmark, 57. 885 Second Ave
☎ 223-4545

Dominican Republic, 53.
1501 Broadway ☎ 768-2480

Ecuador, 69. 800 Second Ave
☎ 808-0170

Egypt, 20. 1110 Second Ave
☎ 759-7120

El Salvador, 91. 46 Park Ave
☎ 889-3608

Estonia, 79. 600 Third Ave
☎ 883-0636

Finland, 36. 866 UN Plaza ☎ 750-4400

France, 8. 934 Fifth Ave ☎ 606-3600

Germany, 37. 871 UN Pl ☎ 940-0400

Great Britain, 28. 845 Third Ave
☎ 745-0200

Greece, 4. 69 E 79th St ☎ 988-5500

Grenada, 69. 800 Second Ave
☎ 599-0301

Guatemala, 90. 57 Park Ave
☎ 686-3837

Guyana, 98. 370 7th Ave
☎ 947-5110

Haiti, 85. 271 Madison Ave
☎ 697-9767

Honduras, 99. 35 W 35th St
☎ 714-9481

Hungary, 29. 223 E 52nd St
☎ 752-0669

Iceland, 43. 800 Third Ave
☎ 593-2700

India, 17. 3 E 64th St ☎ 774-0600

Indonesia, 13. 5 E 68th St
☎ 879-0600

Ireland, 27. 345 Park Ave
☎ 319-2562

Israel, 69. 800 Second Ave
☎ 499-5400

Italy, 12. 690 Park Ave ☎ 737-9100

Jamaica, 56. 767 Third Ave
☎ 935-9000

Japan, 45. 299 Park Ave ☎ 371-8222

Kuwait, 65. 321 E 44th St ☎ 973-4318

Lebanon, 6. 9 E 76th St ☎ 744-7905

Malaysia, 68. 313 E 43rd St
☎ 490-2722

Malta, 87. 249 E 35th St ☎ 725-2345

Mexico, 96. 27 E 39th St ☎ 217-6400

Morocco, 95. 10 E 40th St
☎ 758-2625

Myanmar, 5. 10 E 77th St ☎ 535-1310

Nepal, 67. 820 Second Ave
☎ 370-3988

Netherlands, 35. 1 Rockefeller Plaza
☎ 246-1429

New Zealand, 76. 222 E 41st St
☎ 832-7420

Nicaragua, 67. 820 Second Ave
☎ 986-6562

Nigeria, 66. 828 Second Ave
☎ 808-0301

Norway, 38. 825 Third Ave
☎ 421-7333

Pakistan, 15. 12 E 65th St
☎ 879-5800

Paraguay, 71. 211 E 43rd St
☎ 682-9441

Peru, 42. 241 E 49th St
☎ 646/735-3828

Philippines, 48. 556 Fifth Ave
☎ 764-1330

Airlines

Terminals

Airlines	JFK	LA GUARDIA	NEWARK
Aer Lingus ☎ 800/474-7424	4		
Aeroflot ☎ 888/340-6400	3		
Aerolineas Argentinas ☎ 800/333-0276	4		
Aeromar ☎ 877/237-6627	1		
AeroMexico ☎ 800/237-6639	1		
Aerosvit Ukranian Airlines ☎ 888/661-1620	4		
Air Canada ☎ 888/247-2262	7	CTB-A	A
Air China ☎ 800/982-8802	1		
Air France ☎ 800/237-2747	1		B
Air India ☎ 212/751-6200	4		B
Air Jamaica ☎ 800/523-5585	4		B
Air Malta ☎ 800/756-2582	4		
AirTran Airways ☎ 800/247-8726		CTB-B	A
Air Ukraine ☎ 212/230-1001	4		
Alaska Airlines ☎ 800/426-0333			A
Alitalia ☎ 800/223-5730	1		B
All Nippon Airways ☎ 800/235-9262	7		
America West ☎ 800/235-9292	7	CTB-B	A
American ☎ 800/433-7300	8, 9	CTB-D	A
American Eagle ☎ 800/433-7300	9	CTB-C	
American Trans Air (ATA) ☎ 800/435-9282	4	CTB-B	A
Austrian Airlines ☎ 800/843-0002	1		
Avianca ☎ 800/284-2622	4		
Biman Bangladesh ☎ 212/808-4477	4		
British Airways ☎ 800/247-9297	7		B
BWIA ☎ 800/538-2942	4		
Can Jet ☎ 800/809-7777		CTB-A	
Cathay Pacific ☎ 800/233-2742	7		
China Airlines ☎ 800/227-5118	3		
Colgan Air ☎ 800/428-4322		US Airways	
Continental ☎ 800/525-0280	4	CTB-A	A,C
Continental Connection ☎ 800/525-0280	4		

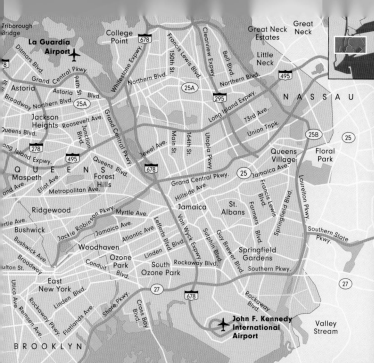

Airlines

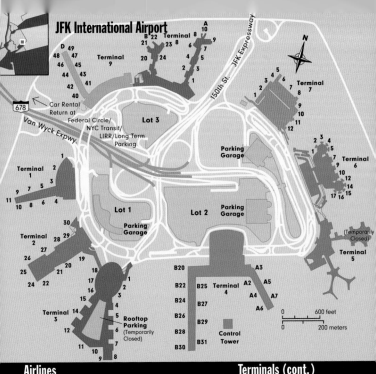

Airlines

Terminals (cont.)

Airlines	JFK	LAGUARDIA	NEWARK
Mexicana ☎ 800/531-7921		CTB-B	B
Midwest ☎ 800/452-2022		CTB-B	B
North American ☎ 800/371-6297	4		B
Northwest ☎ 800/225-2525	4	Delta	B
Olympic ☎ 800/223-1226	1		
Pakistan ☎ 212/760-8455	4		
Qantas ☎ 800/227-4500	7		A
Royal Air Maroc ☎ 800/344-6726	1		
Royal Jordanian ☎ 212/949-0050	3		
SAS ☎ 800/221-2350			B
Saudi Arabian ☎ 718/551-3020	2		
Singapore Airlines ☎ 800/742-3333	4		B
Song ☎ 800/FLY-SONG	2	Delta	
South African Airways ☎ 800/722-9675	3		
Spirit ☎ 800/772-7117		CTB-B	
Sun Country ☎ 800/FLY-NSUN	3		
Swiss ☎ 877/359-7947			B
Tarom-Romanian ☎ 212/560-0840	4		
TACA International ☎ 800/535-8780	4		
TAP Air Portugal ☎ 800/221-7370	4		B
Thai Airways ☎ 800/426-5204	7,4		
Turkish Airlines ☎ 212/339-9650	1		
United ☎ 800/241-6522	7	CTB-B	A
United Express ☎ 800/241-6522		CTB-C	A
Universal ☎ 718/441-4900	4		
US Airways ☎ 800/428-4322		US Airways	A
US Airways Express ☎ 800/428-4322		US Airways	A
US Airways Shuttle ☎ 800/428-4322		US Airways Shuttle	
Uzbekistan Airways ☎ 212/245-1005	4		
Varig ☎ 800/468-2744	4		
Virgin Atlantic ☎ 800/862-8621	4		B

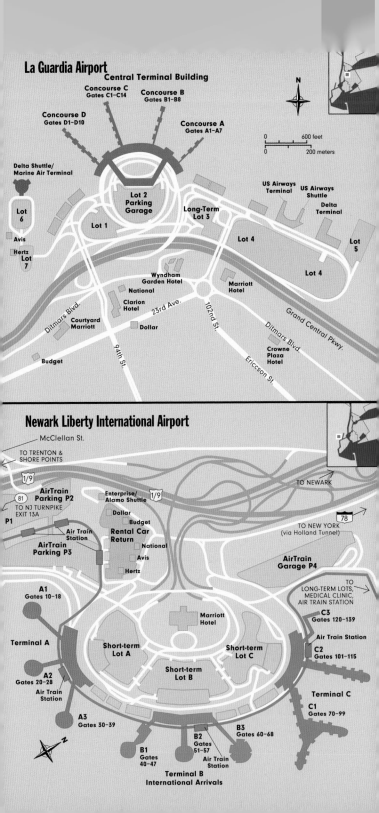

La Guardia Airport

Central Terminal Building

Concourse C
Gates C1–C14

Concourse B
Gates B1–B8

Concourse D
Gates D1–D10

Concourse A
Gates A1–A7

N

0   600 feet
0   200 meters

Delta Shuttle/
Marine Air Terminal

Lot
6

Avis

Hertz
Lot
7

Lot 1

Lot 2
Parking
Garage

Long-Term
Lot 3

US Airways
Terminal

US Airways
Shuttle

Delta
Terminal

Lot 4

Lot 5

Lot 4

Wyndham
Garden Hotel

National

Marriott
Hotel

Clarion
Hotel

Ditmars Blvd.

Courtyard
Marriott

23rd Ave.

Dollar

102nd St.

Grand Central Pkwy.

Ditmars Blvd

Crowne
Plaza
Hotel

Ericsson St.

Budget

94th St.

Newark Liberty International Airport

McClellan St.

TO TRENTON &
SHORE POINTS

1/9

81

AirTrain
Parking P2

TO NJ TURNPIKE
EXIT 13A

P1

Enterprise/
Alamo Shuttle

1/9

Dollar

Budget

TO NEWARK

78

TO NEW YORK
(via Holland Tunnel)

Air Train
Station

AirTrain
Parking P3

Rental Car
Return

National

Avis

Hertz

AirTrain
Garage P4

A1
Gates 10–18

Marriott
Hotel

TO
LONG-TERM LOTS,
MEDICAL CLINIC,
AIR TRAIN STATION

C3
Gates 120–139

Air Train Station

C2
Gates 101–115

Terminal A

Short-term
Lot A

Short-term
Lot C

Short-term
Lot B

A2
Gates 20–28

Air Train
Station

Terminal C

C1
Gates 70–99

A3
Gates 30–39

B3
Gates 60–68

N

B2
Gates
51–57

B1
Gates
40–47

Air Train
Station

Terminal B
International Arrivals

Sloatsburg

PORT JERVIS LINE

Spring Valley

Suffern

N E W

ROCKLAND

Nanuet

Mahwah

Pearl River

Ramsey

Montvale

Park Ridge

Woodcliff Lake

Allendale

MAIN LINE

Waldwick

Hillsdale

Ho-Ho-Kus

Westwood

Ridgewood

BERGEN

Glen Rock   Glen Rock

Emerson

PASCACK VALLEY LINE

BERGEN LINE

Oradell

Hawthorne

N E W   J E R S E Y   **MAIN LINE**

Radburn-Fairlawn

River Edge

Lincoln Park

Mountain View/Wayne

Broadway-Fairlawn

North Hackensack

Towaco

Paterson

Plauderville

Hackensack/Anderson St.

Boonton

Little Falls

Hackensack/Essex St.

Mountain Lakes

Great Notch

Clifton

Teterboro

MONTCLAIR/BOONTON LINE

Montclair Heights

Passaic

Mount Tabor

Mountain Ave.

Delawanna

Wood-Ridge

Upper Montclair

Garfield

Rutherford-East Rutherford

Morris Plains

Watchung Ave.

Walnut St.

ESSEX

Lyndhurst

MORRISTOWN LINE

Bay St.

Kingsland

Morristown

Glen Ridge

Bloomfield

Grand Central Terminal

Convent Station

Brick Church

Watsessing

Secaucus Junction

Penn Station

Madison

Orange

Highland Ave.

East Orange

Broad St.

Newark

Hoboken

33rd St.

Chatham

Mountain Station

South Orange

Penn Station/Newark

Pavonia

MANHATTAN

Maplewood

Harrison

Journal Square

Grove St.

World Trade Center

Summit

Millburn

Short Hills

Newark Liberty International Airport

Exchange Place

Murray Hill

New Providence

North Elizabeth

PATH

Flatbush Ave.

GLADSTONE BRANCH

UNION

Union

Elizabeth

HUDSON

Berkeley Heights

Roselle Park

Upper New York Bay

Cranford

St George

Garwood

Stadium (game days only)

Tompkinsville

Fanwood

Westfield

Stapleton

Netherwood

Clifton

Plainfield

Linden

STATEN ISLAND

Grasmere

RARITAN VALLEY LINE

Metropark

Rahway

Old Town

Dongan Hills

Dunellen

Avenel

Grant City

Jefferson Ave.

AMTRAK

Woodbridge

Oakwood Heights

New Dorp

Metuchen

Great Kills

Bay Terrace

New Brunswick

Edison

Perth Amboy

Annandale

Eltingville

STATEN ISLAND RAPID TRANSIT

Prince's Bay

Huguenot

Lower New York Bay

Nassau

Pleasant Plains

NORTHEAST CORRIDOR LINE

South Amboy

Atlantic

Tottenville

Richmond Valley

Jersey Ave.

MIDDLESEX

Raritan Bay

NORTH JERSEY COAST LINE

Aberdeen-Matawan

MONMOUTH

Hazlet

Middletown

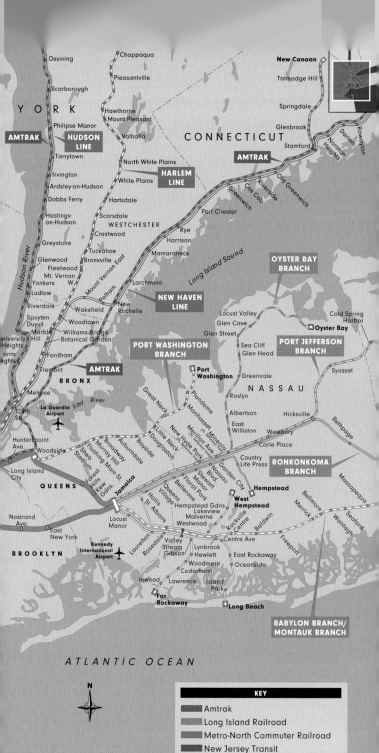

Ossining
Chappaqua
New Canaan
Scarborough
Pleasantville
Talmadge Hill
Springdale
Y O R K
Hawthorne
Mount Pleasant
Glenbrook
Darien
Rowayton
Philipse Manor
Valhalla
C O N N E C T I C U T
Stamford
Noroton
Heights
AMTRAK
**HUDSON
LINE**
Tarrytown
North White Plains
AMTRAK
Irvington
White Plains
**HARLEM
LINE**
Old Greenwich
Ardsley-on-Hudson
Hartsdale
Riverside
Cos Cob
Dobbs Ferry
Scarsdale
Greenwich
Hastings-
on-Hudson
W E S T C H E S T E R
Port Chester
Crestwood
Greystone
Rye
Glenwood
Tuckahoe
Harrison
**OYSTER BAY
BRANCH**
Fleetwood
Bronxville
Mamaroneck
Mt. Vernon
W.
Mount Vernon East
Cold Spring
Harbor
Yonkers
Long Island Sound
Locust Valley
Ludlow
Pelham
Larchmont
Glen Cove
◇ **Oyster Bay**
Riverdale
Wakefield
Glen Street
Spuyten
Duyvil
New
Rochelle
**NEW HAVEN
LINE**
Sea Cliff
**PORT JEFFERSON
BRANCH**
Woodlawn
Glen Head
Marble
Hill
Williams Bridge
Botanical Garden
Syosset
niversity
Heights
**PORT WASHINGTON
BRANCH**
Greenvale
orris
ights
Fordham
▢ **Port
Washington**
N A S S A U
Tremont
Plandome
Roslyn
AMTRAK
Great Neck
Manhasset
B R O N X
Melrose
Albertson
Hicksville
La Guardia
Airport
East
River
Bayside
Little Neck
Merillon Ave.
New Hyde Park
Mineola
East
Williston
Westbury
Bethpage
125th
St.
Auburndale
Carle Place
Huntspoint
Ave.
Broadway
Murray Hill
Flushing Main St.
Douglaston
Nassau
Blvd.
Country
Life Press
Stewart
Manor
**RONKONKOMA
BRANCH**
Woodside
Shea
Stadium
Floral
Park
Garden City
Massapequa
Long Island
City
Kew
Gdns.
Bellerose
Hempstead
Forest
Hills
Jamaica
Queens
Village
Hollis
Hempstead Gdns
**West
Hempstead**
Bellmore
Merrick
Hempstead
Q U E E N S
St. Albans
Lakeview
Nostrand
Ave.
Locust
Manor
Malverne
Westwood
Rockville
Centre
Baldwin
Seaford
Wantagh
East
New York
Freeport
Laurelton
Valley
Stream
Centre Ave.
Kennedy
International
Airport
Rosedale
Gibson
Lynbrook
Hewlett
East Rockaway
B R O O K L Y N
Woodmere
Cedarhurst
Oceanside
Inwood
Lawrence
Island
Park
Far
Rockaway
▢ **Long Beach**
**BABYLON BRANCH/
MONTAUK BRANCH**
A T L A N T I C   O C E A N
N
KEY
Amtrak
Long Island Railroad
Metro-North Commuter Railroad
New Jersey Transit
PATH (Port Authority Trans-Hudson)
Staten Island Rapid Transit
0   10 miles
0   15 km

TIMES SQ
42 ST/GRAND CENTRAL
42 ST/8 AVE
42 ST/ 6 AVE
34 ST/ PENN STN
34 ST/ HERALD SQ
33 ST
28 ST
28 ST
28 ST
23 ST
23 ST
23 ST
18 ST
14 ST/8 AVE
6 AVE
14 ST/ UNION SQ
14 ST
14 ST
3 AVE
8 ST/ NYU
ASTOR PL
CHRISTOPHER ST/ SHERIDAN SQ
W 4 ST/ WASH SQ
BLEECKER ST
BROADWAY/LAFAYETTE E
PRINCE ST
HOUSTON ST
SPRING ST
SPRING ST
BOWERY
CANAL ST
CANAL ST
NEW JERSEY
CANAL ST
Hudson River
FRANKLIN ST
BROOKLYN BR/ CITY HALL
CHAMBERS ST
CITY HALL
PARK PLACE
WORLD TRADE CENTER
BROADWAY/ NASSAU
CORTLANDT ST (CLOSED)
FULTON ST
CORTLANDT ST
WALL ST
RECTOR ST
RECTOR ST
J Z BROAD ST
BOWLING GREEN
WHITEHALL/SOUTH FERRY
SOUTH FERRY

0   1500 feet
0   500 meters

KEY
Subway line
Terminal
Express stop
Local stop
Express and local stop
Free transfer (Local)
Free transfer (Express)

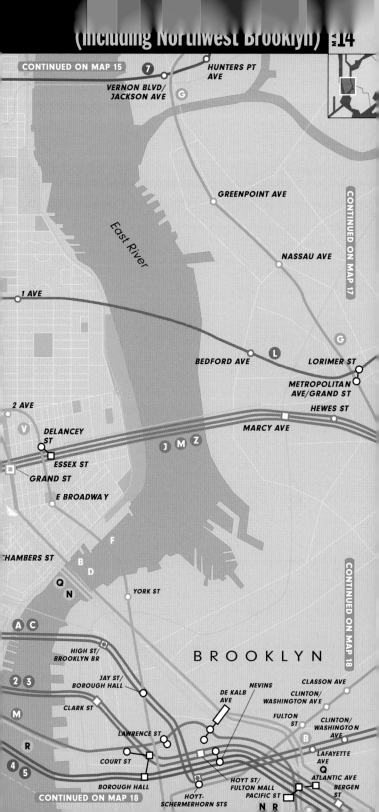

CONTINUED ON MAP 15

7

HUNTERS PT AVE

VERNON BLVD/ JACKSON AVE

G

GREENPOINT AVE

CONTINUED ON MAP 17

NASSAU AVE

East River

1 AVE

G

BEDFORD AVE

L

LORIMER ST

METROPOLITAN AVE/GRAND ST

HEWES ST

2 AVE

MARCY AVE

V

DELANCEY ST

J M Z

ESSEX ST

GRAND ST

E BROADWAY

F

CHAMBERS ST

B

D

Q

N

YORK ST

A C

BROOKLYN

HIGH ST/ BROOKLYN BR

2 3

JAY ST/ BOROUGH HALL

CLASSON AVE

DE KALB AVE

NEVINS

CLINTON/ WASHINGTON AVE

CLARK ST

M

FULTON ST

CLINTON/ WASHINGTON AVE

R

LAWRENCE ST

B

LAFAYETTE AVE

4 5

COURT ST

Q

ATLANTIC AVE

BERGEN ST

BOROUGH HALL

HOYT/ FULTON MALL PACIFIC ST

CONTINUED ON MAP 18

HOYT- SCHERMERHORN STS

N R

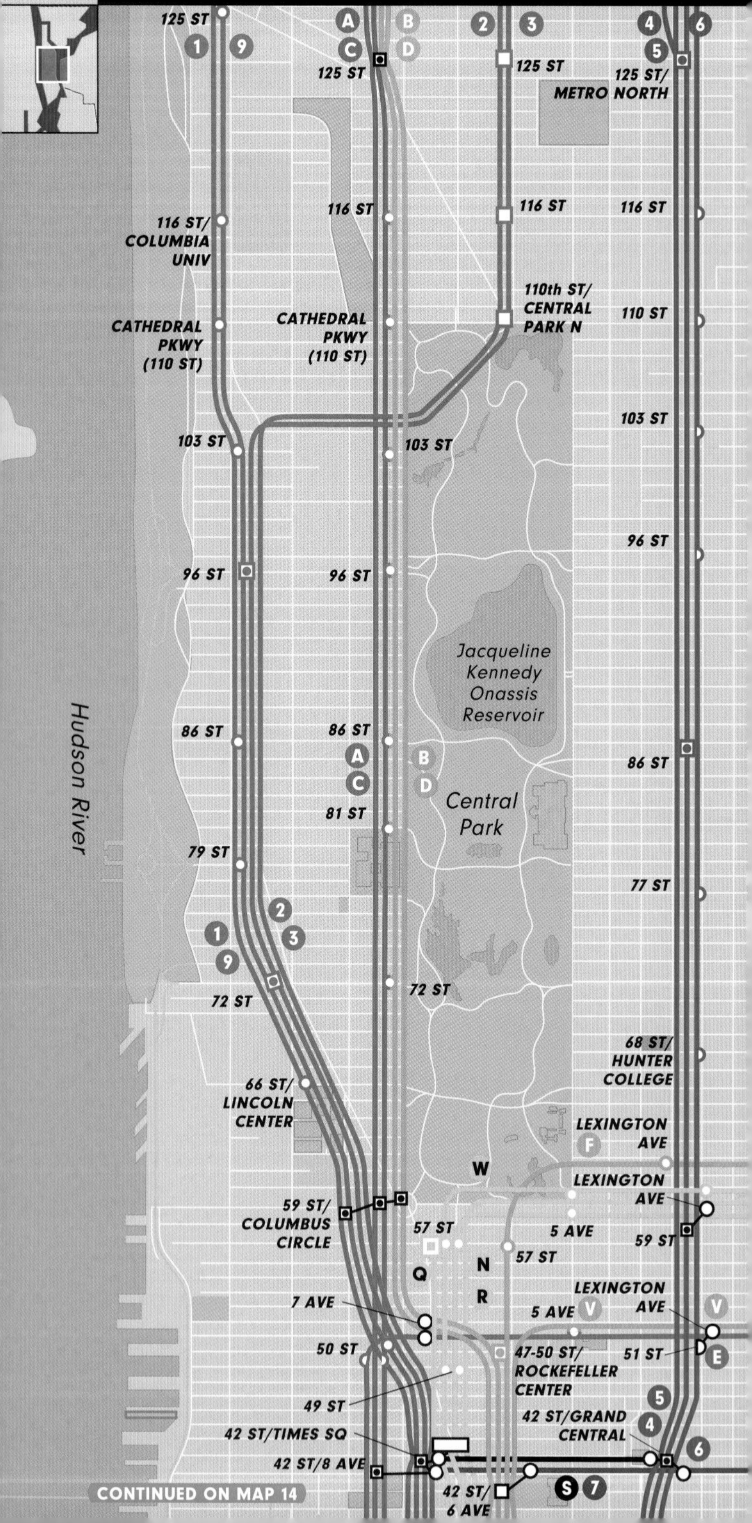

125 ST
125 ST
125 ST
125 ST/
METRO NORTH

116 ST
116 ST
116 ST
116 ST

116 ST/
COLUMBIA UNIV

110th ST/
CENTRAL
PARK N

110 ST

CATHEDRAL
PKWY
(110 ST)

CATHEDRAL
PKWY
(110 ST)

103 ST
103 ST
103 ST

96 ST
96 ST
96 ST

Jacqueline
Kennedy
Onassis
Reservoir

86 ST
86 ST
86 ST

81 ST

Central
Park

79 ST

77 ST

72 ST
72 ST

68 ST/
HUNTER
COLLEGE

66 ST/
LINCOLN
CENTER

LEXINGTON
AVE

LEXINGTON
AVE

59 ST/
COLUMBUS
CIRCLE

57 ST

5 AVE

57 ST

59 ST

W

Q

N
R

LEXINGTON
AVE

7 AVE

5 AVE

50 ST

47-50 ST/
ROCKEFELLER
CENTER

51 ST

49 ST

42 ST/GRAND
CENTRAL

42 ST/TIMES SQ

42 ST/8 AVE

42 ST/
6 AVE

Hudson River

CONTINUED ON MAP 14

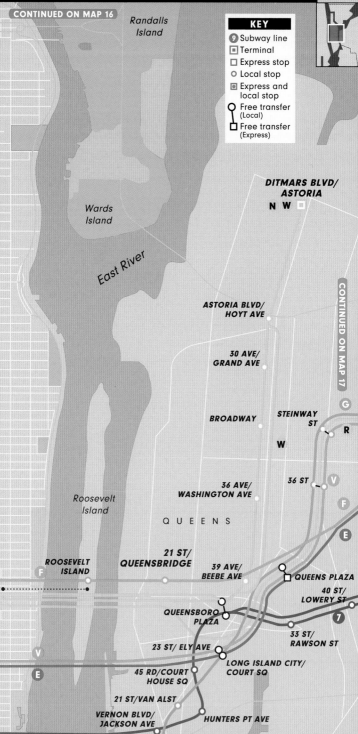

CONTINUED ON MAP 16

Randalls
Island

KEY
- 9 Subway line
- ■ Terminal
- □ Express stop
- ○ Local stop
- ▣ Express and local stop
- Free transfer (Local)
- Free transfer (Express)

Wards
Island

East River

CONTINUED ON MAP 17

DITMARS BLVD/ ASTORIA
N W ■

ASTORIA BLVD/ HOYT AVE

30 AVE/ GRAND AVE

BROADWAY

STEINWAY ST

G

W

R

36 ST

V

F

36 AVE/ WASHINGTON AVE

E

Roosevelt
Island

Q U E E N S

21 ST/ QUEENSBRIDGE

39 AVE/ BEEBE AVE

F **ROOSEVELT ISLAND**

□ **QUEENS PLAZA**

40 ST/ LOWERY ST

○ ○

QUEENSBORO PLAZA

7

33 ST/ RAWSON ST

V

23 ST/ ELY AVE

E

LONG ISLAND CITY/ COURT SQ

45 RD/COURT HOUSE SQ

21 ST/VAN ALST

VERNON BLVD/ JACKSON AVE

HUNTERS PT AVE

G

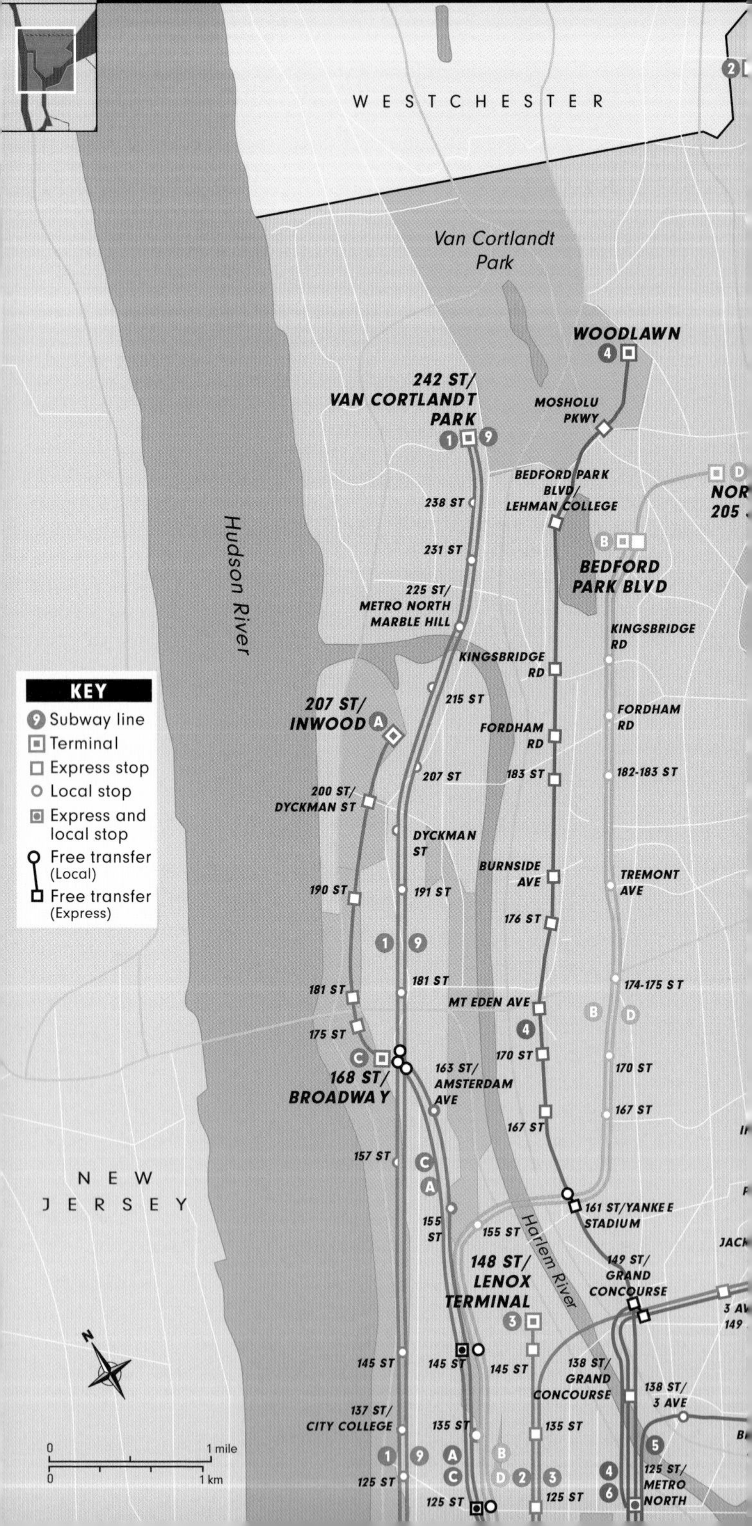

MAP **40** Subways/Bronx & Northern Manhattan

WESTCHESTER

Van Cortlandt Park

WOODLAWN
4 □

MOSHOLU PKWY

242 ST/ VAN CORTLANDT PARK
1 □ 9

BEDFORD PARK BLVD/ LEHMAN COLLEGE

D
NOR 205

238 ST

231 ST

B □ □
BEDFORD PARK BLVD

225 ST/ METRO NORTH MARBLE HILL

KINGSBRIDGE RD

KINGSBRIDGE RD

207 ST/ INWOOD A

215 ST

FORDHAM RD

FORDHAM RD

207 ST

183 ST

182-183 ST

200 ST/ DYCKMAN ST

DYCKMAN ST

BURNSIDE AVE

TREMONT AVE

190 ST

191 ST

176 ST

1 9

181 ST

181 ST

174-175 S

MT EDEN AVE

B D

175 ST

4

170 ST

170 ST

168 ST/ BROADWAY

163 ST/ AMSTERDAM AVE

167 ST

167 ST

157 ST

C
A

161 ST/YANKE E STADIUM

NEW JERSEY

155 ST

155 ST

149 ST/ GRAND CONCOURSE

JACK

148 ST/ LENOX TERMINAL

Harlem River

3 AV 149

3 □

145 ST

145 ST

145 ST

138 ST/ GRAND CONCOURSE

138 ST/ 3 AVE

137 ST/ CITY COLLEGE

135 ST

135 ST

5

125 ST/ METRO NORTH

1 9   A   125 ST   4

125 ST   C   D 2 3   125 ST   6

KEY
- 9 Subway line
- □ Terminal
- □ Express stop
- ○ Local stop
- ▣ Express and local stop
- ○ Free transfer (Local)
- □ Free transfer (Express)

Hudson River

0 ___ 1 mile
0 ___ 1 km

N

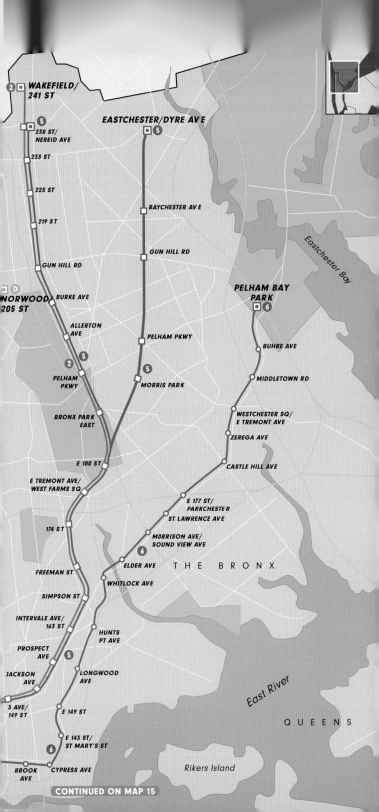

② ▢ **WAKEFIELD/ 241 ST**

② ▢ 238 ST/ NEREID AVE

233 ST

225 ST

219 ST

GUN HILL RD

▢ **NORWOOD/ 205 ST**

BURKE AVE

ALLERTON AVE

② ⑤ PELHAM PKWY

BRONX PARK EAST

E 180 ST

E TREMONT AVE/ WEST FARMS SQ

174 ST

FREEMAN ST

SIMPSON ST

INTERVALE AVE/ 163 ST

PROSPECT AVE

⑤ JACKSON AVE

▢ 3 AVE/ 149 ST

E 149 ST

⑥ E 143 ST/ ST MARY'S ST

BROOK AVE

CYPRESS AVE

EASTCHESTER/DYRE AV E

▢ ⑤

BAYCHESTER AV E

GUN HILL RD

PELHAM PKWY

⑤ MORRIS PARK

Eastchester Bay

PELHAM BAY PARK ▢ ⑥

BUHRE AVE

MIDDLETOWN RD

WESTCHESTER SQ/ E TREMONT AVE

ZEREGA AVE

CASTLE HILL AVE

E 177 ST/ PARKCHESTER

ST LAWRENCE AVE

MORRISON AVE/ SOUND VIEW AVE ⑥

ELDER AVE

WHITLOCK AVE

T H E   B R O N X

HUNTS PT AVE

LONGWOOD AVE

East River

Q U E E N S

Rikers Island

CONTINUED ON MAP 15

MAP 17 Subways/Queens & Northeast Brooklyn

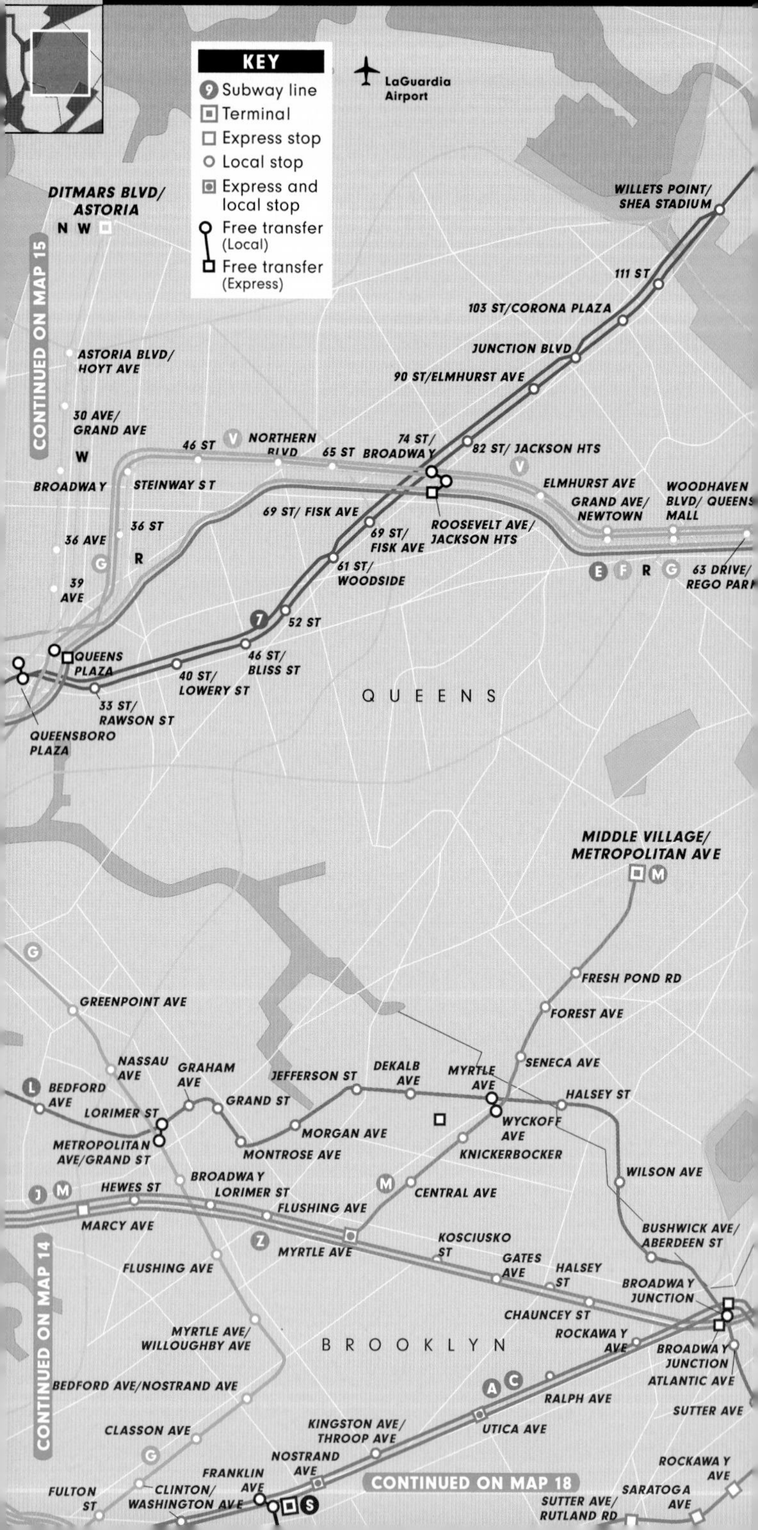

KEY
- Subway line
- Terminal
- Express stop
- Local stop
- Express and local stop
- Free transfer (Local)
- Free transfer (Express)

LaGuardia Airport

CONTINUED ON MAP 15

DITMARS BLVD/ ASTORIA
N W

WILLETS POINT/ SHEA STADIUM

111 ST

103 ST/CORONA PLAZA

JUNCTION BLVD

90 ST/ELMHURST AVE

ASTORIA BLVD/ HOYT AVE

30 AVE/ GRAND AVE
W

46 ST

NORTHERN BLVD

65 ST

74 ST/ BROADWAY

82 ST/ JACKSON HTS

V

ELMHURST AVE
GRAND AVE/ NEWTOWN

WOODHAVEN BLVD/ QUEENS MALL

BROADWAY

STEINWAY ST

36 ST

36 AVE

39 AVE

G

R

69 ST/ FISK AVE

69 ST/ FISK AVE

61 ST/ WOODSIDE

ROOSEVELT AVE/ JACKSON HTS

E F R

63 DRIVE/ REGO PARK

7

52 ST

46 ST/ BLISS ST

40 ST/ LOWERY ST

Queens Plaza

33 ST/ RAWSON ST

Queensboro Plaza

Q U E E N S

MIDDLE VILLAGE/ METROPOLITAN AVE
M

G

FRESH POND RD

FOREST AVE

GREENPOINT AVE

NASSAU AVE

GRAHAM AVE

JEFFERSON ST

DEKALB AVE

MYRTLE AVE

SENECA AVE

HALSEY ST

L

BEDFORD AVE

LORIMER ST

GRAND ST

WYCKOFF AVE

KNICKERBOCKER

WILSON AVE

METROPOLITAN AVE/GRAND ST

MORGAN AVE

MONTROSE AVE

J M

HEWES ST

BROADWAY LORIMER ST

M

CENTRAL AVE

MARCY AVE

FLUSHING AVE

BUSHWICK AVE/ ABERDEEN ST

Z

MYRTLE AVE

KOSCIUSKO ST

GATES AVE

HALSEY ST

BROADWAY JUNCTION

FLUSHING AVE

CHAUNCEY ST

ROCKAWAY AVE

BROADWAY JUNCTION

MYRTLE AVE/ WILLOUGHBY AVE

B R O O K L Y N

ATLANTIC AVE

BEDFORD AVE/NOSTRAND AVE

A C

RALPH AVE

SUTTER AVE

CLASSON AVE

G

KINGSTON AVE/ THROOP AVE

UTICA AVE

ROCKAWAY AVE

FULTON ST

FRANKLIN AVE

NOSTRAND AVE

SARATOGA AVE

CLINTON/ WASHINGTON AVE

S

CONTINUED ON MAP 18

SUTTER AVE/ RUTLAND RD

CONTINUED ON MAP 14

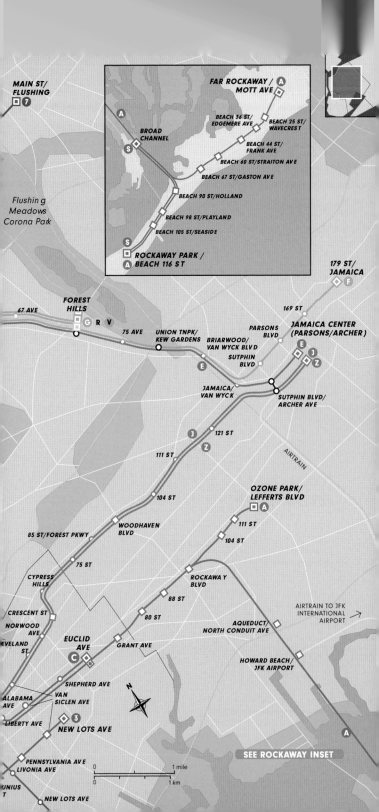

MAIN ST/
FLUSHING

□ **7**

FAR ROCKAWAY /
MOTT AVE

◇ **A**

BEACH 36 ST/
EDGEMERE AVE

BEACH 25 ST/
WAVECREST

A

BROAD
CHANNEL

S

BEACH 44 ST/
FRANK AVE

BEACH 60 ST/STRAITON AVE

BEACH 67 ST/GASTON AVE

BEACH 90 ST/HOLLAND

Flushin g
Meadows
Corona Park

BEACH 98 ST/PLAYLAND

BEACH 105 ST/SEASIDE

S

ROCKAWAY PARK /
BEACH 116 ST

A

179 ST/
JAMAICA

◇ **F**

FOREST
HILLS

67 AVE

□ **G R V**

169 ST

PARSONS
BLVD

JAMAICA CENTER
(PARSONS/ARCHER)

75 AVE

UNION TNPK/
KEW GARDENS

BRIARWOOD/
VAN WYCK BLVD

SUTPHIN
BLVD

◇ **E**

◇ **J Z**

E

JAMAICA/
VAN WYCK

SUTPHIN BLVD/
ARCHER AVE

J

121 ST

Z

111 ST

AIRTRAIN

104 ST

OZONE PARK/
LEFFERTS BLVD

□ **A**

85 ST/FOREST PKWY

WOODHAVEN
BLVD

111 ST

104 ST

75 ST

CYPRESS
HILLS

ROCKAWAY
BLVD

AIRTRAIN TO JFK
INTERNATIONAL
AIRPORT →

CRESCENT ST

88 ST

80 ST

AQUEDUCT/
NORTH CONDUIT AVE

NORWOOD
AVE

EVELAND
ST

EUCLID
AVE

C

GRANT AVE

HOWARD BEACH/
JFK AIRPORT

SHEPHERD AVE

ALABAMA
AVE

VAN
SICLEN AVE

N

3

LIBERTY AVE

NEW LOTS AVE

PENNSYLVANIA AVE

LIVONIA AVE

SEE ROCKAWAY INSET

A

UNIUS
T

NEW LOTS AVE

0   1 mile

0   1 km

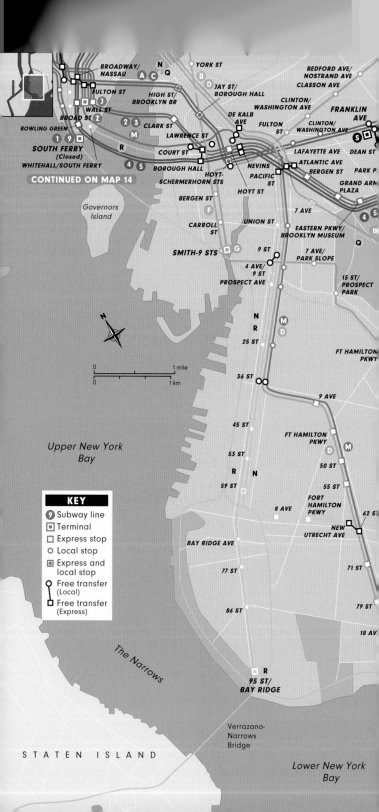

Jacqueline Kennedy Onassis Reservoir

Central Park

W. 86th St.

E. 92nd St.

E. 86th St.

First Ave.
Second Ave.
York Ave.

West End Ave.
Amsterdam Ave.

W. 79th St. Boat Basin

E. 79th St.
Roosevelt Island

LONG ISLAND CITY

The Lake

E. 79th St.

W. 72nd St.

Broadway

Riverside Dr.

Columbus Ave.

Central Park W.

Third Ave.
Lexington Ave.

E. 73rd St.
E. 72nd St.
E. 71st St.

9A

UPPER WEST SIDE

Tenth Ave.

Ninth Ave.

Fifth Ave.
Madison Ave.
Park Ave.

UPPER EAST SIDE

E. 65th St.

East River
FDR Dr.

Vernon Blvd.

The Pond

Central Park S.

E. 63rd St.
E. 62nd St.
E. 61st St.

E. 59th St.

Queensboro Bridge

QUEENS

W. 57th St.

W. 56th St.
W. 54th St.
W. 52nd St.
W. 51st St.
W. 50th St.
W. 49th St.
W. 48th St.
W. 47th St.
W. 46th St.
W. 45th St.
W. 44th St.
W. 43rd St.
W. 42nd St.
W. 41st St.

W. 50th St.

Eighth Ave.

E. 57th St.

MIDTOWN

TURTLE BAY

E. 53rd St.

E. 48th St.
E. 47th St.

E. 42nd St.

495

W. 39 St./Javits Center

Lincoln Tunnel

E. 42nd St.

Queens-Midtown Tunnel

THEATER DISTRICT

11th Ave.

495

W. 34th St.

E. 37th St.

E. 34th St.

GREEN-POINT

MURRAY HILL

W. 29th St.

W. 30th St.

Ninth Ave.
Eighth Ave.
Seventh Ave.
Ave. of the Americas
Fifth Ave.
Madison Ave.
Park Ave. S.
Lexington Ave.
Third Ave.
Second Ave.
First Ave.

E. 25th St.

W. 24th St.
W. 23rd St.

W. 26th St.

CHELSEA

GRAMERCY

E. 23rd St.

E. 20th St.

East River
FDR Dr.

W. 18th St.
W. 16th St.
W. 15th St.
W. 14th St.

E. 14th St.

Ave. C

Hudson River Park

Hudson River

WEST VILLAGE

Fourth Ave.

Ave. A
Ave. B
Ave. D

Horatio St.

W. 12th St.

GREENWICH VILLAGE

EAST VILLAGE

E. Houston St.

W. 11th St.

Christopher St.

NOHO

LOWER EAST SIDE

West Side Hwy.
Varick St.

Clarkson St.
W. Houston St.

Bowery

Williamsburg Bridge

NEW JERSEY

SOHO

Broadway

Delancey St.

Grand St.

Holland Tunnel

DOWNTOWN

LITTLE ITALY

Cherry St.

HOBOKEN

Vestry St.
Laight St.
N. Moore St.

Canal St.

TRIBECA

CHINATOWN

Montgomery St.

Manhattan Bridge

Flatbush Ave.

Chambers St.

Civic Center

278

JERSEY CITY

World Trade Center Site

FINANCIAL DISTRICT

Brooklyn Bridge

SOUTH STREET SEAPORT

Brooklyn Bridge

BROOKLYN

BATTERY PARK CITY

Whitehall St.

State St.

Battery Park

Brooklyn-Battery Tunnel

Brooklyn Queens Expwy.

BROOKLYN HEIGHTS

N

MAP 21 Buses/Manhattan below 14th Street

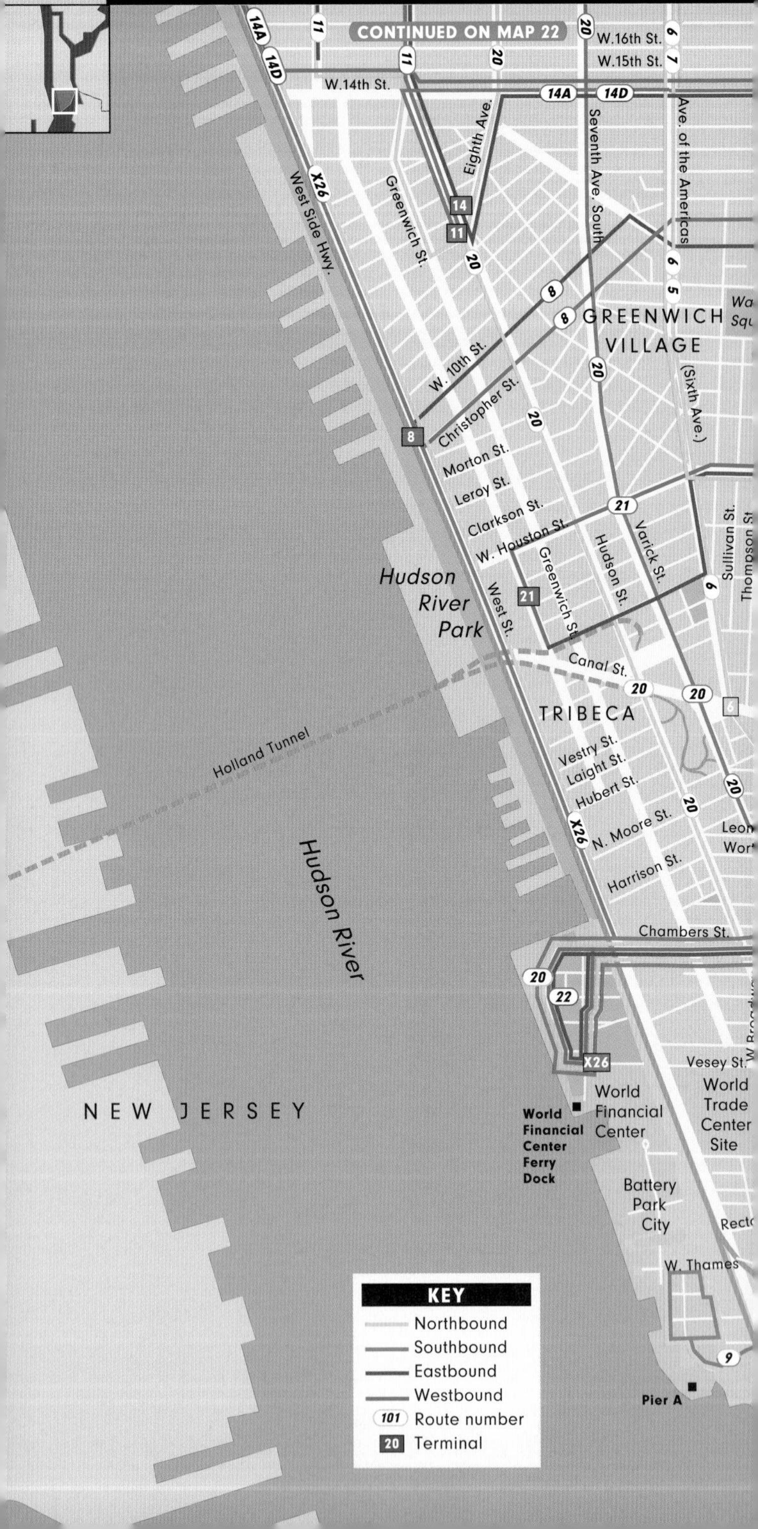

CONTINUED ON MAP 22

W.16th St.
W.15th St.
W.14th St.

Eighth Ave.

Seventh Ave. South

Ave. of the Americas

West Side Hwy.

Greenwich St.

X26

14A 14D

14A 14D

11

11

14

11

20

8

8

GREENWICH VILLAGE

Wa
Squ

20

(Sixth Ave.)

W. 10th St.

Christopher St.

8

Morton St.

Leroy St.

Clarkson St.

W. Houston St.

20

21

Varick St.

Hudson St.

Sullivan St.

Thompson St

Hudson River Park

West St.

21

Greenwich St.

6

Canal St.

20

20

TRIBECA

Holland Tunnel

Vestry St.
Laight St.
Hubert St.

X26

N. Moore St.

20

20

20

Leon
Wor

Harrison St.

Hudson River

Chambers St.

20

22

NEW JERSEY

X26

Vesey St.

W Broadwa

World Financial Center Ferry Dock

World Financial Center

World Trade Center Site

Battery Park City

Recto

W. Thames

9

Pier A

KEY	
	Northbound
	Southbound
	Eastbound
	Westbound
101	Route number
20	Terminal

MAP 22 Buses/Manhattan 14th St–72nd St

CONTINUED ON MAP 23

Central Park

Central Park S.

CONTINUED ON MAP 21

W. 72nd St.

W. 70th St.

W. 68th St.

W. 66th St.

W. 65th St.

W. 60th St.

W. 58th St.

W. 57th St.

W. 55th St.

W. 53rd St.

W. 50th St.

W. 49th St.

W. 47th St.

W. 44th St.

W. 42nd St.

Lincoln Tunnel

W. 38th St.

W. 36th St.

W. 34th St.

W. 32nd St.

W. 30th St.

W. 28th St.

W. 25th St.

W. 23rd St.

CHELSEA

W. 21st St.

W. 18th St.

W. 15th St.

W. 14th St.

Hudson River

Henry Hudson Pkwy.

West End Ave.

Amsterdam Ave.

Tenth Ave.

Ninth Ave.

Eleventh Ave.

Eighth Ave.

Seventh Ave.

Broadway

Ave. of the Americas

(Sixth Ave.)

West Side Hwy.

9A

495

57 72 104 10 66 20 11 7 5 6 30 31 27 16 4 X26 Q32 23 14 14A 14D 50 42 34

MAP 23 **Buses/Manhattan 72nd St–125th St**

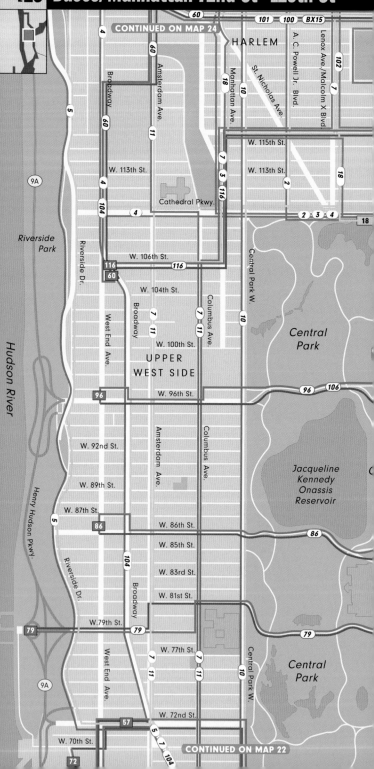

CONTINUED ON MAP 24

HARLEM

Broadway
Amsterdam Ave.
Manhattan Ave.
St. Nicholas Ave.
A. C. Powell Jr. Blvd.
Lenox Ave./Malcolm X Blvd.

W. 115th St.
W. 113th St.
W. 113th St.
Cathedral Pkwy.

Riverside Park
Riverside Dr.

W. 106th St.
W. 104th St.
Columbus Ave.
Central Park W.

Central Park

W. 100th St.

UPPER WEST SIDE

West End Ave.
Broadway

W. 96th St.

W. 92nd St.
Amsterdam Ave.
Columbus Ave.

Jacqueline Kennedy Onassis Reservoir

W. 89th St.
W. 87th St.
W. 86th St.
W. 85th St.
W. 83rd St.
W. 81st St.

Hudson River

Henry Hudson Pkwy.
Riverside Dr.

W. 79th St.

W. 77th St.

Central Park W.

Central Park

W. 72nd St.

W. 70th St.

CONTINUED ON MAP 22

MARBLE HILL

BX12 BX20

100

Inwood Hill Park

9A

BX12

BX12

Tenth Ave.

207th St.

BX20

Broadway

204th Ave.

Dyckman St.

Nagle Ave.

4

Fort Tryon Park

W. Fordham Rd.

1

87

1

95

Cross Bronx Expwy.

Henry Hudson Pkwy.

KEY
— Northbound
— Southbound
— Eastbound
— Westbound
101 Route number
20 Terminal

3 101

St. Nicholas Ave.

Amsterdam Ave.

Harlem River Dr.

98 BX7

100

Broadway

FORT WASHINGTON

4 98

BX3 BX13 BX35

W. 181st St.

BX3, BX11, BX13, BX35, BX36

BX11 BX36

W. 179th St.

5 W. 178th St.

98

THE BRONX

Third Ave.

95 1

To George Washington Bridge

4

3

101

Audubon Ave.

Melrose Ave.

WASHINGTON HEIGHTS

100

Fort Washington Ave.

W. 168th St.

2 W. 167th St.

18 W. 166th St.

St. Nicholas Ave.

Edgecombe Ave.

N

Grand Concourse

BX7

4

5

Broadway

Riverside Dr.

W. 157th St.

E. 161st St.

Major Deegan Expwy.

0 1500 feet
0 500 meters

BX6

10

BX6

3 W. 155th St.

BX6

Harlem River

Eugenio Maria de Hostos Blvd.

4 5

101 100

10

18

1 7 102 W. 147th St.

98

MANHATTANVILLE

BX19 W. 145th St.

BX19

11

River Bank State Park

Riverside Dr.

Amsterdam Ave.

101 100

102 7

Third Ave.

Willis Ave.

BX33

E. 138th St.

Hudson River

Henry Hudson Pkwy.

18

W. 139th St.

Lenox Ave./Malcolm X Blvd.

1

BX33

87

Harlem River Dr.

Bruckner Blvd.

W. 135th St.

BX33

BX35

9A

BX15

W. 135th St.

Convent Ave.

3

F. Douglass Blvd.

A. C. Powell Jr.

10

2

1

E. 128th St.

BX15

BX15 W. 125th St.

104

60

Broadway

104

Amsterdam Ave.

60

18

St. Nicholas Ave.

Blvd.

101 100

102 7

Madison Ave.

35

15

E. 127th St.
E. 125th St.

BX15 60

35

15

Morningside Ave.

98

Lexington Ave.

Third Ave.

Second Ave.

First Ave.

5

60

HARLEM

Marcus Garvey Park

101

1

EAST HARLEM

E. 116th St.

11

CONTINUED ON MAP 23

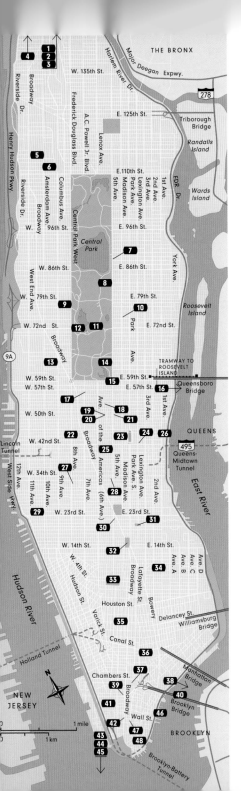

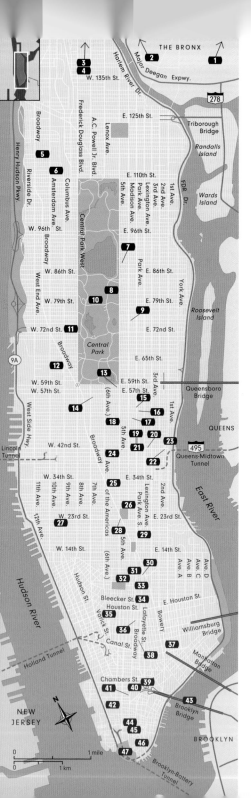

Mosques

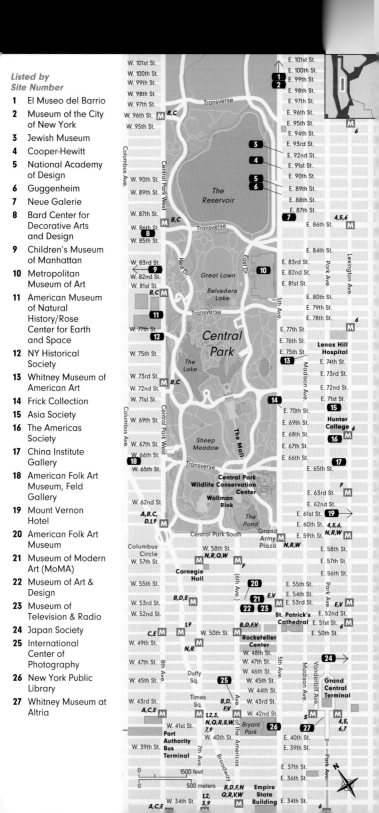

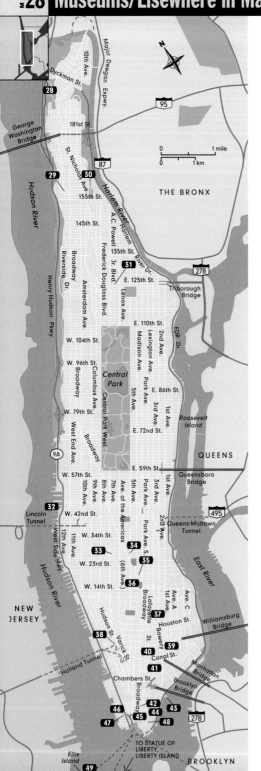

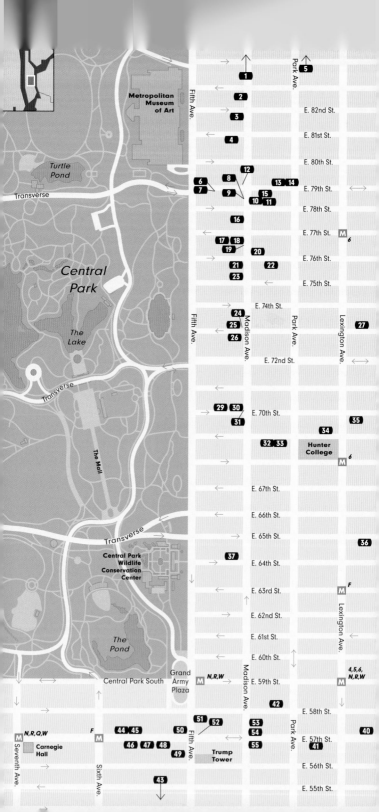

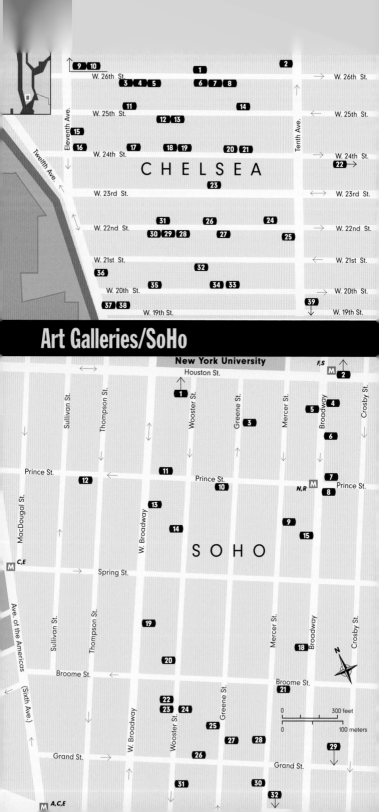

Art Galleries/SoHo

Chelsea Galleries
Listed by Site Number

1 Team
2 Paul Kasmin
3 Tony Shafrazi
4 Stephen Haller
5 Lehmann Maupin
6 Galerie Lelong
7 Caren Golden
7 Clementine
7 Greene Naftali
7 Henry Urbach Architecture
7 Nicole Klagsburn
8 Robert Miller
9 Sean Kelly
10 Ceres
11 Cheim & Reid
12 PaceWildenstein
13 Viridian Artists
14 Klotz-Sirmon
14 McKenzie
14 SoHo 20
15 Fischbach
15 Robert Mann
16 Gagosian
17 Mary Boone
18 Luhring Augustine
19 Andrea Rosen
20 Metro Pictures
21 Barbara Gladstone
22 Sepia
23 Van de Weghe
24 Max Protech
25 Fredericks-Freiser
26 D'Amelio Terras
26 DCA
26 303
27 Matthew Marks
28 Brent Sikkema
29 Sandra Gering
30 Sonnabend
31 Julie Saul
31 Leslie Tonkonow
31 Yancey Richardson
32 Paula Cooper
33 Jack Shainman
34 ACA
34 Ricco/Maresca
35 Feigen Contemporary
36 Ariel Meyerowitz
37 David Zwirner
38 Postmasters
39 Bellwether

Soho Galleries
Listed by Site Number

1 Grey
2 Leica
3 Phyllis Kind
4 American Primitive
5 June Kelly
6 Westwood
7 Luise Ross
7 Susan Teller
8 Cavin-Morris
8 Lennon Weinberg
8 Nolan/Eckman
8 Peter Freeman
8 Staley-Wise
9 Suite 106
10 Mimi Ferzt
11 Meisel
12 Ward-Nasse
13 Nancy Hoffman
14 Peter Blum
15 Margarete Roeder
16 Sragow
17 Storefront for Art & Architecture
18 Swiss Institute
19 OK Harris
20 Brooke Alexander
21 Dieu Donné Papermill
22 Spencer Brownstone
23 The Drawing Center
24 The Drawing Room
25 Woodward
26 Deitch Projects
27 Artists Space
28 55 Mercer
29 Art in General
30 Ronald Feldman
31 Deitch Projects
32 Grant

Chelsea Galleries
Listed Alphabetically

SoHo Galleries
Listed Alphabetically

American Primitive, 6.
594 Broadway ☎ 966–1530

Art in General, 29. 79 Walker St
☎ 219–0473

Artists Space, 27. 38 Greene St
☎ 226–3970

Brooke Alexander, 20.
59 Wooster St ☎ 925–4338

Cavin-Morris, 8. 560 Broadway
☎ 226–3768

Deitch Projects, 26. 76 Grand St
☎ 343–7300

Deitch Projects, 31. 26 Wooster St
☎ 343–7300

Dieu Donné Papermill, 21.
433 Broome St ☎ 226–0573

The Drawing Center, 23.
35 Wooster St ☎ 219–2166

The Drawing Room, 29.
40 Wooster St ☎ 219–2166

55 Mercer, 28. 55 Mercer St
☎ 226–8513

Grant, 32. 7 Mercer St ☎ 343–2919

Grey, 1. 100 Washington Sq E
☎ 998–6780

June Kelly, 7. 591 Broadway
☎ 226–1660

Leica, 2. 670 Broadway ☎ 777–3051

Lennon Weinberg, 8. 560 Broadway
☎ 941–0012

Luise Ross, 7. 568 Broadway
☎ 343–2161

Margarete Roeder, 15.
545 Broadway ☎ 925–6098

Meisel, 11. 141 Prince St ☎ 677–1340

Mimi Ferzt, 10. 114 Prince St
☎ 343–9377

Nancy Hoffman, 13.
429 W Broadway ☎ 966–6676

Nolan/Eckman, 8. 560 Broadway
☎ 925–6190

OK Harris, 19. 383 W Broadway
☎ 431–3600

Peter Blum, 14. 99 Wooster St
☎ 343–0441

Peter Freeman, 8. 560 Broadway
☎ 966–5154

Phyllis Kind, 3. 136 Greene St
☎ 925–1200

Ronald Feldman, 30. 31
Mercer St
☎ 226–3232

Spencer Brownstone, 22.
39 Wooster St ☎ 334–3455

Sragow, 16. 73 Spring St
☎ 219–1793

Staley-Wise, 8. 560 Broadway
☎ 966–6223

Storefront for Art & Architecture, 17.
97 Kenmare St ☎ 431–5795

Suite 106, 9. 112 Mercer St
☎ 274–9166

Susan Teller, 7. 568 Broadway
☎ 941–7335

Swiss Institute, 18. 495 Broadway
☎ 925–2035

Ward-Nasse, 12. 178 Prince St
☎ 925–6951

Westwood, 6. 578 Broadway
☎ 925–5700

Woodward, 25. 476 Broome St
☎ 966–3411

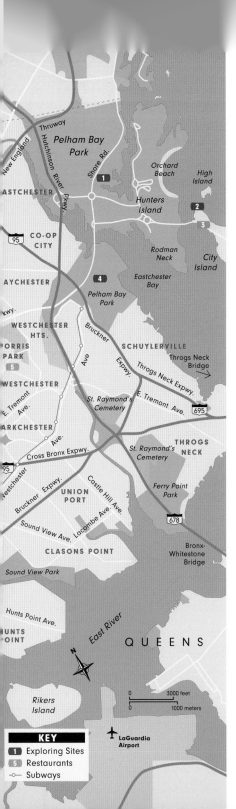

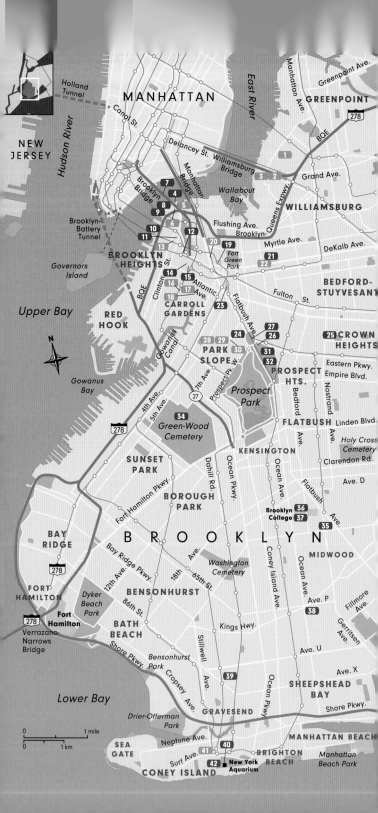

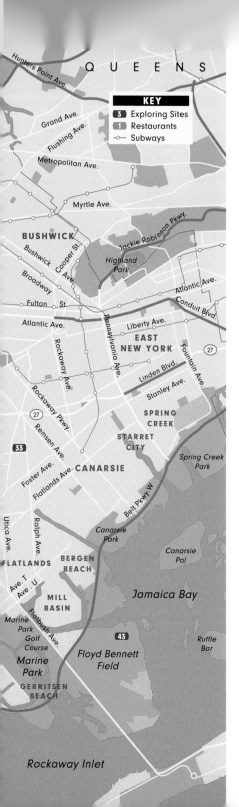

Queens Listed by Site Number

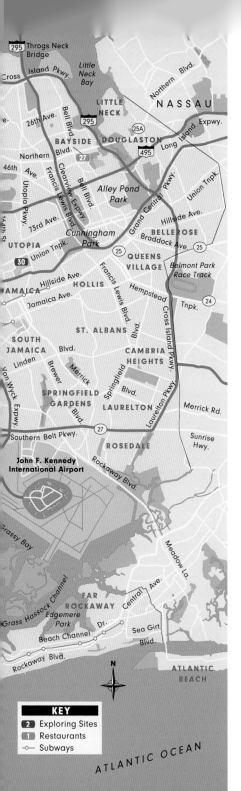

KEY
- **2** Exploring Sites
- **1** Restaurants
- −o− Subways

ATLANTIC OCEAN

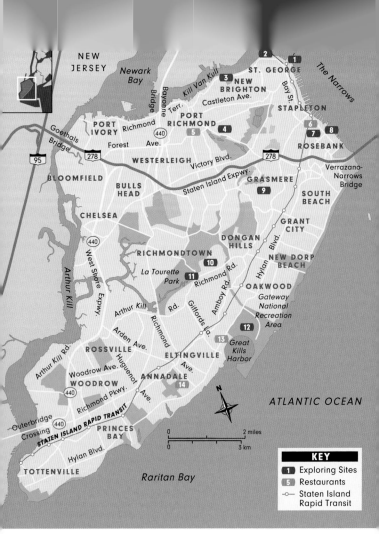

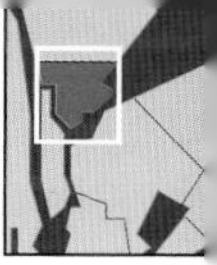

BRONX SITES

Arthur Ave Italian Market, 26.
Arthur Ave, betw E Fordham Rd &
E Tremont Ave

Bartow-Pell Mansion, 1.
895 Shore Rd N & Pelham Bay Pkwy
☎ 718/885-1461

Bronx County Courthouse, 28.
851 Grand Concourse ☎ 718/590-3640

Bronx Museum of the Arts, 27.
1040 Grand Concourse ☎ 718/681-6000

Bronx Zoo (IWCP), 6. Fordham Rd &
Bronx River Pkwy ☎ 718/367-1010

Christ Church, 10. Henry Hudson Pkwy
& 252nd St ☎ 718/543-1011

City Island, 2. Long Island Sound

Creston Ave Baptist Church, 19.
114 E 188th St ☎ 718/367-1754

Edgar Allan Poe Cottage, 20.
Grand Concourse & E Kingsbridge Rd
☎ 718/881-8900

Edgehill Church, 16.
2550 Independence Ave ☎ 718/549-7324

**Enrico Fermi Cultural Center/Library,
21.** 610 E 186th St ☎ 718/933-6410

Fordham University, 22.
441 E Fordham Rd ☎ 718/817-1000

Henry Hudson Memorial, 15.
Independence Ave & W 227th St

Kingsbridge Armory, 8.
Kingsbridge Rd & Jerome Ave

Manhattan College, 13.
Manhattan College Pkwy & W 242nd St
☎ 718/862-8000

NY Botanical Garden, 7. Southern
Blvd & 200th St ☎ 718/817-8700

Pelham Bay Park, 4. Pelham Bay

Roberto Clemente State Park, 18.
W Tremont Ave & Matthewson Rd
☎ 718/299-8750

**Van Cortlandt House Museum,
12.** B'way & W 246th St
☎ 718/543-3344

Wave Hill, 9. W 249th St &
Independence Ave ☎ 718/549-3200

World War I Memorial Tower, 14.
Riverdale Ave & 239th St

BRONX RESTAURANTS

Bellavista Cafe, 11. 554 W 235th St
☎ 718/548-2354. Italian. $-$$

Dominick's, 24. 2335 Arthur Ave
☎ 718/733-2807. Italian. ¢-$$$

Enzo's, 5. 1998 Williamsbridge Rd
☎ 718/409-3828. Italian. $

Jimmy's Bronx Cafe, 17.
281 W Fordham Rd ☎ 718/329-2000.
Pan-Latin. $-$$

Le Refuge Inn, 3. 620 City Island Ave
☎ 718/885-2478. French. $$$$

Mario's, 23. 2342 Arthur Ave
☎ 718/584-1188. Italian. $-$$

Press Café, 29. 114 E 157th St
☎ 718/401-0545. Italian. ¢-$

Roberto's, 25. 632 E 186th St
☎ 718/733-9503. Italian. $$-$$$

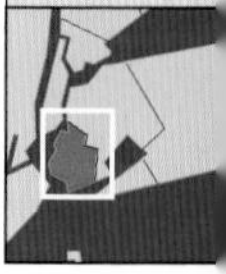

BROOKLYN SITES

Bargemusic, Ltd, 6. Fulton Ferry
Landing, Old Fulton St & Waterfront
☎ 718/624-2083

Bklyn Acad of Music (BAM), 23.
30 Lafayette Ave ☎ 718/636-4100

Bklyn Borough Hall, 15.
209 Joralemon St ☎ 718/802-3700

Bklyn Botanic Garden, 33. 1000
Washington Ave ☎ 718/623-7200

Bklyn Bridge, 3. Cadman Plaza,
Bklyn, to City Hall Park, Manhattan

**Bklyn Center for Performing
Arts, 37.** Brooklyn College,
2900 Campus Rd ☎ 718/951-4500

Bklyn Children's Museum, 29.
145 Brooklyn Ave ☎ 718/735-4400

Bklyn College CUNY, 36. 2900
Bedford Ave ☎ 718/951-5000

MAP **32**

$$$$ = *over $35* $$$ = *$28-$35* $$ = *$19-$27* $ = *$11-$18*   ¢ = *under $10*
Based on cost per person for an entrée.

BROOKLYN SITES (cont.)

Brooklyn Historical Society, 11.
128 Pierrepont St ☎ 718/222-4111

Brooklyn Museum of Art, 31.
200 Eastern Pkwy ☎ 718/638-5000

Brooklyn Public Library, 26.
Grand Army Plaza ☎ 718/230-2100

Coe House, 35. 1128 E 34th St

Coney Island Amusement Park, 42.
1000 Surf Ave ☎ 718/372-0275

Fulton Ferry Pier, 8. Foot of Old Fulton St

Gateway National Recreation Area, 43. Floyd Bennett Field, Flatbush Ave & Shore Pkwy ☎ 718/338-3799

Green-Wood Cemetery, 34.
Fifth Ave & 25th St ☎ 718/768-7300

Long Island Univ, 19. Univ Plaza,
DeKalb & Flatbush Aves
☎ 718/488-1011

Montauk Club, 24. 25 Eighth Ave
☎ 718/638-0800

NY Aquarium, 40. Boardwalk & W 8th St
☎ 718/265-FISH

NY Transit Museum, 14. Boerum Pl &
Schermerhorn St ☎ 718/694-5100

Old Gravesend Cemetery, 39.
Gravesend Neck Rd & MacDonald Ave

Pratt Institute, 21. 200 Willoughby Ave
☎ 718/636-3600

The Promenade, 10. Between
Montague & Clark Sts

St Ann's Warehouse, 4.
38 Water St ☎ 718/254-8779

Soldiers' & Sailors' Memorial Arch, 27.
Flatbush Ave & Eastern Pkwy

State St Houses, 15. 290-324 State St

Wyckoff House/Pieter Claesen, 33.
5816 Clarendon Rd ☎ 718/629-5400

Wyckoff-Bennett Homestead, 38.
1669 E 22nd St

BROOKLYN RESTAURANTS

al di la, 30. 248 Fifth Ave
☎ 718/783-4565. Italian. $

Banania Cafe, 16. 241 Smith St
☎ 718/237-9100. French. $

Blue Ribbon Brooklyn, 28. 280 Fifth
Ave ☎ 718/840-0404. Eclectic. $-$$

Cucina, 29. 256 Fifth Avenue
☎ 718/230-0711. Italian. $$

Diner, 3. 85 Broadway
☎ 718/486-3077. American. ¢-$

Gargiulo's Restaurant, 41.
2911 W 15th St ☎ 718/266-4891. Italian.
¢-$$$

Grimaldi's Pizzeria, 6.
19 Old Fulton St ☎ 718/858-4300.
Pizza. $-$$

The Grocery, 18. 288 Smith St
☎ 718/596-3335. American. $$$

Henry's End, 13. 44 Henry St
☎ 718/834-1776. New American. $-$$

Junior's Restaurant, 20. 386 Flatbush
Ave ☎ 718/852-5257. American. ¢-$$$

Madiba, 22. 195 DeKalb Ave
☎ 718/855-9190. South African. $-$$

Oznot's Dish, 1. 79 Berry St
☎ 718/599-6596. Middle Eastern. $

Peter Luger Steak House, 2. 178 B'way
☎ 718/387-7400. Steak. $$$$

River Cafe, 5. 1 Water St
☎ 718/522-5200. Contemporary. $$$$

Saul, 17. 140 Smith St ☎ 718/935-9844.
Contemporary. $-$$

QUEENS SITES

**American Museum of the
Moving Image, 7.** 35th Ave &
36th St ☎ 718/784-0077

Bowne House, 21.
37-01 Bowne St ☎ 718/359-0528

Court House Square, 4.
45th Ave & 21st St

**Flushing Meadows-Corona
Park, 17.** College Point Blvd & Grand
Central Pkwy ☎ 718/760-6565

Fort Tilden, 33. Breezy Pt,
Gateway NRA ☎ 718/318-4300

Friends Meeting House, 22.
137-16 Northern Blvd ☎ 718/358-9636

Hunter's Point Historic District, 5.
45th Ave & 21st-23rd Sts

Isamu Noguchi Garden Museum, 8.
9-01 33rd Rd ☎ 718/204-7088

Jacob Riis Park, 32. Marine Bridge
Pkwy at Rockaway Pt Blvd,
Gateway NRA ☎ 718/318-4300

Jamaica Bay Wildlife Refuge, 31.
Broad Channel & First Rd,
Gateway NRA ☎ 718/318-4340

Louis Armstrong House, 12.
34-56 107th St ☎ 718/478-8274

Kissena Park, 26.
Rose Ave & Parsons Blvd

QUEENS SITES (cont.)

Museum for African Art, 6.
36-01 43rd Ave ☎ 718/784-7700

NY Hall of Science, 15. 47-01 111th St
☎ 718/699-0005

PS 1 Contemporary Art Center, 2.
22-25 Jackson Ave ☎ 718/784-2084

Queens Botanical Gardens, 24.
43-50 Main St ☎ 718/886-3800

Queens Historical Society, 20.
143-35 37th Ave ☎ 718/939-0647

Queens Museum of Art, 16. Flushing
Meadows-Corona Park ☎ 718/592-9700

Socrates Sculpture Park, 9.
32-01 Vernon Blvd ☎ 718/956-1819

St John's University, 30.
8000 Utopia Pkwy ☎ 718/990-2000

Weeping Beech Tree, 23.
37th Ave & Parsons Blvd

West Side Tennis Club, 29.
1 Tennis Pl ☎ 718/268-2300

QUEENS RESTAURANTS

Elias Corner, 11. 24-02 31st St
☎ 718/932-1510. Greek Seafood. $

Green Field, 13. 108-01
Northern Blvd
☎ 718/672-5202. Brazilian. $$

Jackson Diner, 14. 37-47 74th St
☎ 718/672-1232. Indian. ¢-$$

Joe's Shanghai, 25. 136-21 37th Ave
☎ 718/539-3838. Chinese $-$$

Manducatis, 3. 13-27 Jackson Ave
☎ 718/729-4602. Italian. $-$$

Mombar, 10. 25-22 Steinway St
☎ 718/726-2356. Middle Eastern.
$-$$

Penang, 18. 38-04 Prince St
☎ 718/321-2078. Malaysian. ¢-$

Ping's Seafood, 28.
83-02 Queens Blvd ☎ 718/396-1238.
Chinese. ¢-$$

Shanghai Tide, 19.
135-20 40th Rd ☎ 718/661-4234.
Chinese. ¢-$

Uncle Jack's Steakhouse, 27.
39-40 Bell Blvd ☎ 718/229-1100.
Steak. $$$$

Water's Edge Restaurant, 1.
44th Dr at Vernon Blvd
☎ 718/482-0033. American. $-$$$$

STATEN ISLAND SITES

Alice Austin House Museum, 8.
2 Hylan Blvd ☎ 718/816-4506

Garibaldi-Meucci Museum, 7.
420 Tompkins Ave ☎ 718/442-1608

**Gateway National Recreation
Area, 12.** Fort Wadsworth
☎ 718/354-4500

**Historic Richmondtown/Staten
Island Historical Society, 11.**
441 Clarke Ave ☎ 718/351-1611

**Jacques Marchais Museum of
Tibetan Art, 10.** 338 Lighthouse Ave
☎ 718/987-3500

Snug Harbor Cultural Center, 3.
1000 Richmond Ter ☎ 718/448-2500

Staten Island Botanical Garden, 3.
1000 Richmond Terrace
☎ 718/273-8200

Staten Island Ferry, 1.
St George Terminal, Richmond
Terrace & Hyatt St ☎ 718/815-2628

**Staten Island Institute of Arts
& Sciences, 2.** 75 Stuyvesant Pl
☎ 718/727-1135

MAP **34**

Staten Island Zoo, 4.
614 Broadway ☎ 718/442-3100

STATEN ISLAND RESTAURANTS

Aesop's Tables, 6. 1233 Bay St
☎ 718/720-2005. New American.
$-$$$

Angelina's, 14. 26 Jefferson Blvd
☎ 718/227-7100. Italian. $$-$$$

Carol's Cafe, 13. 1571 Richmond Rd
☎ 718/979-5600. Eclectic. $$-$$$

Denino's Pizzeria, 5.
524 Port Richmond Ave
☎ 718/442-9401. Pizza. ¢-$

Marina Cafe, 13. 154 Mansion Ave
☎ 718/967-3077. Seafood. $-$$

$$$$ = *over $35* $$$ = *$28-$35* $$ = *$19-$27* $ = *$11-$18*   ¢ = *under $10*
Based on cost per person for an entrée.

MARBLE HILL

Kingsbridge Rd.

Grand Concourse

Bronx River

Bronx Park

Baker Field

INWOOD

Isham Park

207th St.

Tenth Ave.

Inwood Hill Park

9A

UNIVERSITY HTS

Broadway

Dyckman St.

TREMONT

Tremont Ave.

1

95

Fort Tryon park

Nagle Ave.

Highbridge Park

St. Nicholas Ave.

Harlem River Dr.

Amsterdam Ave.

MORRIS HTS

Crotona Park

Fort Washington Park

Broadway

WASHINGTON HEIGHTS

W. 181st St.

Cross Bronx Expwy.

Claremont Park

Third Ave.

Boston Rd.

95 1

J. Hood Wright Park

Audubon Ave.

University Ave.

MORRISANIA

George Washington Bridge

Fort Washington Ave.

St. Nicholas Ave.

Broadway

Highbridge Park

HIGH BRIDGE

87

John Mullaly Park

Grand

THE BRONX

Melrose Ave.

E. 163rd St.

Westchester Ave.

Macombs Dam Park

E. 161st St.

MELROSE

Concourse

W. 155th St.

Trinity Cemetery

Fort Washington Park

Jackie Robinson Park

Edgecombe Ave.

Franz Sigel Park

Major Deegan

0   1500 feet
0   500 meters

Eugenio Maria de Hostos Blvd.

St. Mary's Park

Southern Blvd.

Bruckner Blvd.

Hudson River

Riverbank State Park

Henry Hudson Pkwy.

Riverside Dr.

Amsterdam Ave.

Convent Ave.

W. 145th St.

Colonel Young Park

Frederick Douglass Blvd.

Adam Clayton Powell Jr. Blvd.

Harlem River

Harlem River Dr.

MOTT HAVEN

Willis Ave.

Third Ave.

E. 138th St.

PORT MORRIS

St. Nicholas Park

W. 135th St.

W. 138th St.

Lenox Ave. / Malcolm X Blvd.

Expwy.   Bruckner   Blvd.

87

278

Sheltering Arms Park

Sakura Park

W. 125th St.

MORNINGSIDE HEIGHTS

Morningside Ave.

Manhattan Ave.

St. Nicholas Ave.

Harlem River Drive Park

Randalls Island Park

Riverside Park

Broadway

Amsterdam Ave.

Columbus Ave.

Morningside Park

Cathedral Pkwy.

E. 125th St.

HARLEM

Marcus Garvey Park

Lexington Ave.

EAST HARLEM

Triborough Bridge

278

9A

West End Ave.

Riverside Dr.

W. 106th St.

Central Park W.

Fifth Ave.

Madison Ave.

Park Ave.

E. 110th St.

Thomas Jefferson Park

FDR Dr.

E. 110th St. Recreation Pier

Wards Island Park

East River

Central Park

E. 106th St.

Second Ave.

First Ave.

York Ave.

East River Esplanade

UPPER WEST SIDE

W. 96th St.

Jacqueline Kennedy Onassis Reservoir

E. 96th St.

UPPER EAST SIDE

Carl Schurz Park

QUEENS

W. 86th St.

E. 86th St.

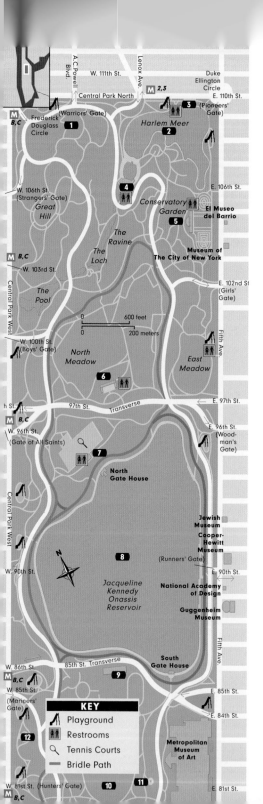

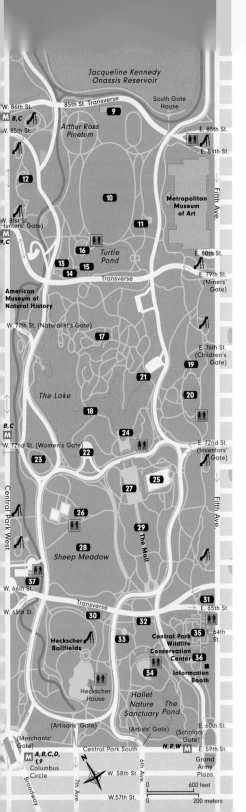

Flushing Bay

Whitestone Expwy.

Northern Blvd.

126th Pl.

127th Pl.

34th Ave.

Grand Central Pkwy.

35th Ave.

127th St.

36th Ave.

Willets Point Blvd.

Shea Stadium

37th Ave.

126th St.

38th Ave.

Van Wyck Expwy.

River

N

39th Ave.

Roosevelt Ave.

M 7

Flushing

678

Corona Rail Road Yard

U.S. Tennis Association Arena/ Arthur Ashe Stadium

Meridian Rd.

Flushing Meadows - Corona Park

0   300 feet

0   100 meters

Shea Stadium & U.S. Tennis Association Arena

Yankee Stadium

E. 162nd St.

P

Jerome   Ave.

Macombs   Dam   Park

E. 162nd St.

P

E. 161st St.

Macombs Dam Bridge Approach

B, D, 4   M   Babe Ruth Plaza

Rupert Pl.

Yankee Stadium

Lou Gehrig Plaza

P

Bronx Boro Hall

Major Deegan Expwy.

Harlem River

E. 157th St.

River Ave.

Gerard Ave.

Walton Ave.

P

E. 153rd St.

P

P

P

P

Grand Concourse

Franz Sigel Park

N

87

0   300 feet

0   100 meters

P

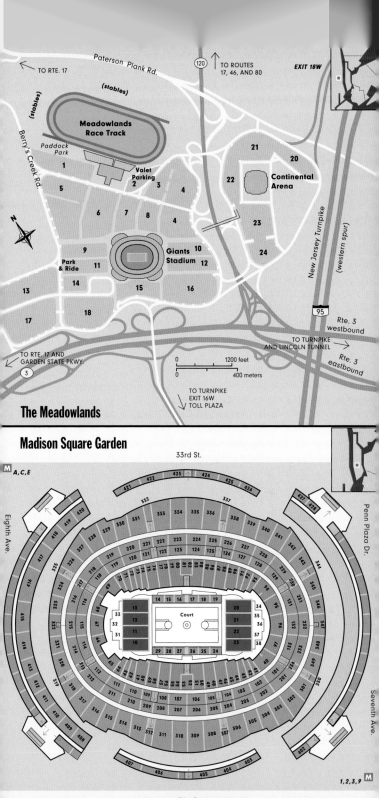

The Meadowlands

Paterson Plank Rd.

TO RTE. 17

(stables)

(stables)

Berry's Creek Rd.

120 TO ROUTES 17, 46, AND 80

EXIT 18W

Meadowlands Race Track

Paddock Park

1

Valet Parking

2   3

5

6   7   8

4

4

9

10

Giants Stadium

12

Park & Ride

11

14

15

16

13

17

18

21

20

22

Continental Arena

23

24

New Jersey Turnpike

(western spur)

95

Rte. 3 westbound

TO TURNPIKE AND LINCOLN TUNNEL

Rte. 3 eastbound

TO RTE. 17 AND GARDEN STATE PKWY.

3

0   1200 feet
0   400 meters

TO TURNPIKE EXIT 16W TOLL PLAZA

Madison Square Garden

33rd St.

M A, C, E

Eighth Ave.

Penn Plaza Dr.

Seventh Ave.

Court

1, 2, 3, 9 M

31st St.

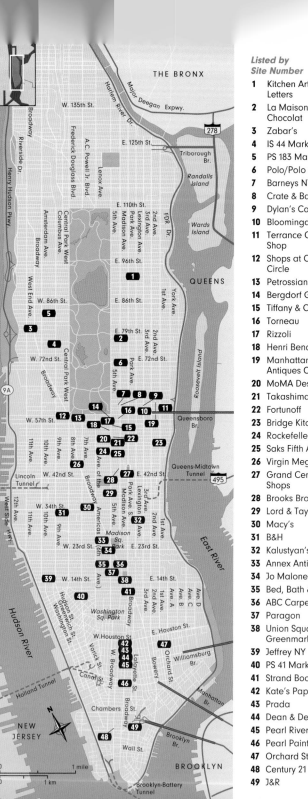

THE BRONX

W. 135th St.

Major Deegan Expwy.

Harlem River Dr.

278

Broadway

Riverside Dr.

Henry Hudson Pkwy.

E. 125th St.

Triborough Br.

Randalls Island

Frederick Douglass Blvd.

A.C. Powell Jr. Blvd.

Lenox Ave.

Wards Island

E. 110th St.

E. 96th St.

5th Ave.

Madison Ave.

Park Ave.

3rd Ave.

2nd Ave.

FDR Dr.

QUEENS

Amsterdam Ave.

Columbus Ave.

Central Park West

Broadway

West End Ave.

1

W. 86th St.

E. 86th St.

York Ave.

1st Ave.

5

3

W. 79th St.

E. 79th St.

2nd Ave.

3rd Ave.

2

4

W. 72nd St.

W. 72nd St.

6

Park Ave.

5th Ave.

Roosevelt Island

11th Ave.

10th Ave.

9th Ave.

Central Park West

Broadway

Columbus Ave.

7 **8** **9**

14

W. 57th St.

12 **13**

18

16 **10** **11**

17

15

19

Queensboro Br.

8th Ave.

7th Ave.

6th Ave.

20 **22**

21

24 **25**

26

23

11th Ave.

10th Ave.

9th Ave.

Lincoln Tunnel

W. 42nd St.

28 **27** E. 42nd St.

Queens-Midtown Tunnel

495

West Side Hwy.

12th Ave.

9A

29

W. 34th St.

30

31

5th Ave.

Madison Ave.

Park Ave.

Lexington Ave.

3rd Ave.

2nd Ave.

1st Ave.

32

Broadway

Ave. of the Americas (6th Ave.)

W. 23rd St.

Madison Sq. Park

E. 23rd St.

33

34

35 **36**

37

39 W. 14th St.

E. 14th St.

38

Ave. A

Ave. B

Ave. C

Ave. D

40

41

Washington Sq. Park

Hudson St.

Greenwich St.

Washington St.

W. Houston St.

E. Houston St.

42
43
44
45

Lafayette St.

Orchard St.

Bowery

47

Williamsburg Br.

Varick Ave.

W. Broadway

46

Canal St.

Hudson River

Holland Tunnel

Chambers St.

Broadway

49

Manhattan Br.

NEW JERSEY

N

48

Wall St.

Brooklyn Br.

Brooklyn-Battery Tunnel

BROOKLYN

0   1 mile

0   1 km

E. 76th St.

9

E. 75th St.

10

Whitney Museum of American Art

11

E. 74th St.

| 0 | 600 feet |
| 0 | 200 meters |

12

E. 73rd St.

Fifth Ave.

Madison Ave.

Park Ave.

N

E. 72nd St.

13

E. 71st St.

14 15

Frick Collection

E. 70th St.

16 17

18

19

E. 69th St.

20

21

Hunter College

E. 68th St.

22 23

E. 67th St.

24 25

Central Park

E. 66th St.

26

27

29 28

30

31 32

E. 65th St.

33

E. 64th St.

34

35

E. 63rd St.

36

37 38

E. 62nd St.

Children's Zoo

Central Park Wildlife Conservation Center

39
40

E. 61st St.

41 42

44 43

45 E. 60th St.

46 47

50

51 52 49

E. 59th St.

Grand Army Plaza

N,R,W

Plaza Hotel

E. 58th St.

Conservatory Water

Central Park

Listed Alphabetically

Alicia Mugetti, 4. 999 Madison Ave
☎ 794-6186, Womenswear

Baccarat, 52.
625 Madison Ave ☎ 826-4100

Bally of Switzerland, 51.
628 Madison Ave ☎ 751-9082, Shoes

Bang & Olufsen, 10.
952 Madison Ave ☎ 879-6161, Audio

Barneys NY, 41.
660 Madison Ave ☎ 826-8900

Barry Friedman Ltd, 25.
32 E 67th St ☎ 794-8950, Antiques

Bottega Veneta, 47.
635 Madison Ave ☎ 371-5511,
Leather Goods

Calvin Klein, 44.
654 Madison Ave ☎ 292-9000

Chanel, 33.
737 Madison Ave. ☎ 535-5505

Chloé, 16.
850 Madison Ave ☎ 717-8220

Christian Louboutin, 11.
941 Madison Ave ☎ 396-1884, Shoes

Cole-Haan, 42.
667 Madison Ave ☎ 421-8440, Shoes

Corner Bookstore, 1.
1313 Madison Ave ☎ 831-3554

Crate & Barrel, 50.
650 Madison Ave. ☎ 308-0011, Home

Crawford Doyle Booksellers, 3.
1082 Madison Ave ☎ 288-6300

Design Within Reach, 38.
27 E 62nd St ☎ 888-4539, Home

Diesel, 48. 770 Lexington Ave.
☎ 308-0055, Jeans

DKNY, 43.
655 Madison Ave ☎ 223-3569

Dolce & Gabbana, 20.
825 Madison Ave ☎ 249-4100

Emanuel Ungaro, 24.
792 Madison Ave ☎ 249-4090

Erica Wilson, 34.
717 Madison Ave ☎ 832-7290,
Needlepoint

Florian Papp, 9. 962 Madison Ave
☎ 288-6770, Antiques

Fred Leighton, 26. 773 Madison Ave
☎ 288-1872, Jewelry

Georg Jensen, 39.
683 Madison Ave ☎ 759-6457

Gianfranco Ferre, 14.
870 Madison Ave ☎ 717-5430,
Clothing

Gianni Versace, 21.
815 Madison Ave ☎ 744-6868

Giorgio Armani, 30.
760 Madison Ave ☎ 988-9191

Givenchy, 35.
710 Madison Ave ☎ 688-4338

Gucci, 18.
840 Madison Ave ☎ 717-2619

Hermès, 37.
691 Madison Ave ☎ 751-3181

Issey Miyake, 8.
992 Madison Ave ☎ 439-7822

Jean Paul Gaultier, 28.
759 Madison Ave ☎ 249-0235

JM Weston, 22. 812 Madison Ave
☎ 535-2100, Mens Shoes

Julie Artisan's Gallery, 29.
762 Madison Ave ☎ 717-5959,
Wearable Art

Krizia, 27.
769 Madison Ave ☎ 879-1211

La Maison du Chocolat, 6.
1018 Madison Ave ☎ 744-7117

La Perla, 23.
803 Madison Ave. ☎ 570-0050

Missoni, 5.
1009 Madison Ave ☎ 517-9339

Mitchel London Foods, 31.
22A E 65th St ☎ 737-2850

Nicole Farhi, 45.
10 E 60th St ☎ 223-8811

Polo/Polo Sport, 13.
867 Madison Ave ☎ 606-2100 and
888 Madison Ave ☎ 434-8000

Reinstein/Ross, 12.
29 E 73rd St ☎ 722-1901, Jewelry

Prada, 17.
841 Madison Ave ☎ 327-4200

Pratesi, 19. 829 Madison Ave
☎ 288-2315, Linens

Sherry-Lehmann Inc, 40.
679 Madison Ave ☎ 838-7500,
Wine

Simon Pearce, 49. 500 Park Ave.
☎ 421-8801, Tableware

Timberland, 36.
709 Madison Ave ☎ 754-0436

Tod's, 46. 650 Madison Ave
☎ 644-5945, Shoes

Valentino, 32.
747 Madison Ave ☎ 772-6969

Vera Wang, 7.
991 Madison Ave ☎ 628-3400

Wicker Garden Children, 2.
1327 Madison Ave ☎ 410-7001

Yves St Laurent, 15.
855 Madison Ave ☎ 988-3821

MAP 42 Shopping/Fifth Avenue & 57th Street

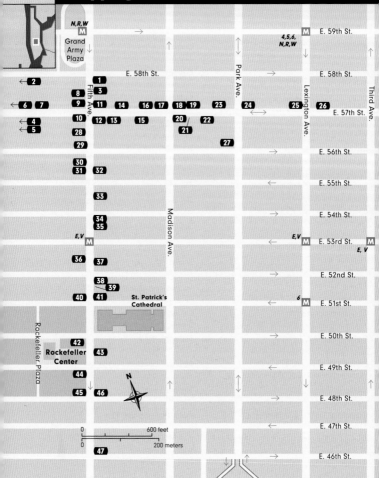

Listed by Site Number

Listed Alphabetically

Alfred Dunhill, 32. 711 Fifth Ave
☎ 753-9292, Cigars

American Girl Place, 46.
604 Fifth Ave ☎ 371-2220, Dolls

Barnes & Noble, 45. 600 Fifth Ave
☎ 765-0592

Bergdorf Goodman, 3. 754 Fifth Ave
☎ 753-7300

Bergdorf Men's, 1. 745 Fifth Ave
☎ 753-7300

Borders Books, 24.
461 Park Ave ☎ 980-6785

Brooks Brothers, 36.
666 Fifth Ave ☎ 261-9440

Buccellati, 22. 46 E 57th St
☎ 308-2900, Jewelry

Bulgari, 10. 730 Fifth Ave
☎ 315-9000, Jewelry

Burberry, 14. 9 E 57th St ☎ 407-7100

Cartier, 38. 653 Fifth Ave ☎ 753-0111

Chanel, 16. 15 E 57th St ☎ 355-5050

Christian Dior, 17. 21 E 57th St
☎ 931-2950

Coach, 18.
595 Madison Ave ☎ 754-0041

Daffy's, 25. 125 E 57th St ☎ 376-4477,
Discount Clothing

Dana Buchman, 23. 65 E 57th St
☎ 319-3257

Fauchon, 27. 442 Park Ave
☎ 308-5919, French Gourmet

Fendi, 29. 720 Fifth Ave ☎ 767-0100

Fortunoff, 35. 681 Fifth Ave
☎ 758-6660, Jewelry/Tableware

Gianni Versace Boutique, 39.
647 Fifth Ave ☎ 317-0224

Gucci, 34. 685 Fifth Ave ☎ 826-2600

H & M, 40. 640 Fifth Ave ☎ 489-8777,
Clothing

H Stern Jewelers, 41. 645 Fifth Ave
☎ 688-0300

Hammacher Schlemmer, 26.
147 E 57th St ☎ 421-9000

Harry Winston, 30. 718 Fifth Ave
☎ 245-2000, Jewelry

Henri Bendel, 31. 712 Fifth Ave
☎ 247-1100

HMV, 47. 565 Fifth Ave ☎ 681-6700,
CDs

Hugo Boss, 3.
717 Fifth Ave ☎ 485-1832, Clothing

Kate's Paperie, 5. 140 W 57th St
☎ 459-0700, Stationery

Lee's Art Shop, 4. 220 W 57th St
☎ 247-0110

Louis Vuitton, 11. 1 E 57th St
☎ 758-8877

Mikimoto, 10. 730 Fifth Ave
☎ 457-4600, Jewelry

Minamoto Kitchoan, 44.
608 Fifth Ave ☎ 489-3747,
Japanese Bakery

NBA Store, 36. 666 Fifth Ave
☎ 515-6221

NikeTown, 13. 6 E 57th St
☎ 891-6453

Otto Tootsi Plohound, 21.
38 E 57th St ☎ 231-3199, Shoes

Petrossian, 2. 911 Seventh Ave
☎ 245-2217, Caviar

Prada, 19. 45 E 57th St ☎ 308-2332

Prada, 28. 724 Fifth Ave ☎ 664-0010

Rizzoli, 7. 31 W 57th St ☎ 759-2424,
Bookstore

Saks Fifth Ave, 43. 611 Fifth Ave
☎ 753-4000

Salvatore Ferragamo, 37.
661 Fifth Ave ☎ 759-3882

Steinway & Sons, 6. 109 W 57th St
☎ 246-1100, Pianos

Takashimaya, 33. 693 Fifth Ave.
☎ 350-0100, Japanese Style

Teuscher Chocolates, 42. 620 Fifth
Ave ☎ 246-4416

Tiffany & Co, 12. 727 Fifth Ave
☎ 755-8000

Torneau, 15. 12 E 57th St ☎ 758-7300,
Watches

Van Cleef & Arpels, 9.
744 Fifth Ave ☎ 644-9500

Victoria's Secret, 20. 34 E 57th St
☎ 758-5592

W. 24th St.
W. 23rd St.
W. 22nd St.
W. 21st St.
W. 20th St.
W. 19th St.
W. 18th St.
W. 17th St.
W. 16th St.
W. 15th St.
W. 14th St.
W. 13th St.
W. 12th St.
W. 11th St.
W. 10th St.
W. 9th St.
W. 8th St.

Madison Square Park
N, R
Flatiron Building

Tenth Ave.
Ninth Ave.
Eighth Ave.
Seventh Ave.
Ave. of the Americas
Fifth Ave.
Broadway

C,E
M
A,C,E,L
M 1,2,3, 9,L
F,L,V
M
F,V
M

Little W. 12th St.
Gansevoort St.
Horatio St.
Jane St.
W. 12th St.
Abingdon Sq.
Bethune St.
Bank St.
W. 11th St.
Perry St.
Charles St.
W. 10th St.
Greenwich Ave.
Waverly Pl.
Milligan Pl.
Patchin Pl.
Gay St.

GREENWICH VILLAGE

Sheridan Sq.
Waverly Pl.
W. Washington Pl.

Hudson River Park
West Side Hwy.
Washington St.
Greenwich St.
Hudson St.
Christopher St.
Grove St.
Commerce St.
Bedford St.
Jones St.
Cornelia St.
Bleecker St.
Sixth Ave.
MacDougal St.
Sullivan St.
LaGuardia Pl.

MacDougal Alley
Washington Mews
Washington Sq. N.
Washington Square Park
Washington Sq. S.
New York University
Minetta La.
Father Demo Sq.
Bleec
W. Houston St.
Carmine St.
Downing St.
St. Luke's Pl.
Barrow St.
Morton St.
Leroy St.

A,B,C, D,E,F,V
M
1,9
M

Listed by Site Number

Listed by Site Number

Listed Alphabetically

Adidas Original Store, 1.
136 Wooster St ☎ 777-2001

Agnès b, 30. 103 Greene St
☎ 925-4649, Womenswear

Alice Underground, 46.
481 Broadway ☎ 431-9067, Vintage

Anna Sui, 31. 113 Greene St
☎ 941-8406, Womenswear

Apple Store, 28. 103 Prince St
☎ 226-3126, Computers

Anthropologie, 40. 375 W Broadway
☎ 343-7070, Womenswear/Home

APC, 27. 131 Mercer St ☎ 966-9685,
Clothing

Area ID Moderne, 14.
262 Elizabeth St ☎ 219-9903, Home

Bloomingdales, 44.
504 Broadway ☎ 729-5900

Boca Grande, 42.
66 Greene St ☎ 334-6120, Home

Broadway Panhandler, 47.
477 Broome St ☎ 966-3434, Kitchen

Ceci-Cela, 21. 55 Spring St
☎ 274-9179, Bakery

Ceramica, 35. 59 Thompson St
☎ 941-1307, Italian Ceramics

Cite, 33. 100 Wooster St ☎ 431-7272,
Antiques

City Barn Antiques, 22.
269 Lafayette St ☎ 941-5757

Costume National, 41.
108 Wooster St ☎ 431-1530, Clothing

Dean & DeLuca, 23. 560 Broadway
☎ 226-6800, Gourmet

D&G, 34. 434 W Broadway
☎ 965-8000, Clothing

DiPalo Fine Foods, 20. 200 Grand St
☎ 226-1033, Italian Foods

Eileen Fisher, 38. 395 W Broadway
☎ 431-4567, Womenswear

Erica Tanov, 17.
204 Elizabeth St ☎ 334-8020

Hilfiger, 39. 372 W Broadway
☎ 917/237-0983

Global Table, 6. 107-109 Sullivan St
☎ 431-5839, Tableware

Jacques Carcanaques, 51.
21 Greene St ☎ 925-8110,
Asian Antiques

Janet Russo, 13. 262 Mott St
☎ 625-3297, Womenswear

Jonathan Adler, 49.
47 Greene St ☎ 941-8950, Pottery

Kate Spade, 43.
454 Broome St ☎ 274-1991, Purses

Kate's Paperie, 24.
561 Broadway ☎ 941-9816

Lâle, 19. 200 Mott St ☎ 941-7641,
Home

Marie Belle, 48. 484 Broome St
☎ 923-6999, Chocolate

Me + Ro, 15. 241 Elizabeth St
☎ 237-9215, Jewelry

Mood Indigo, 5. 181 Prince St
☎ 254-1176, Antique Tableware

Moss, 10. 146 Greene St ☎ 226-2190,
Home

Nancy Koltes, 18. 31 Spring St
☎ 219-2271, Home

Otto Tootsi Plohound, 34.
413 W Broadway ☎ 925-8931, Shoes

Peter Fox, 7. 105 Thompson St
☎ 431-7426, Shoes

Pleats Please, 3. 128 Wooster St
☎ 226-3600, Clothing

Portico, 45. 72 Spring St ☎ 941-7800,
Home

Pottery Barn, 12.
600 Broadway ☎ 219-2420

Prada, 26.
575 Broadway ☎ 334-8888

Robert Lee Morris, 37.
400 W Broadway ☎ 431-9405,
Jewelry

Sean, 2. 132 Thompson St
☎ 598-5980, Menswear

Sephora, 25. 555 Broadway
☎ 625-1309, Cosmetics

Shu Uemura, 9. 121 Greene St
☎ 979-5500, Cosmetics

Sigerson Morrison, 16.
242 Mott St ☎ 941-5404, Shoes

Simon Pearce, 32. 120 Wooster St
☎ 334-2393, Tableware

Sullivan Street Bakery, 36.
73 Sullivan St ☎ 334-9435

Traveler's Choice Bookstore, 52.
2 Wooster St ☎ 941-1535

Troy, 11. 138 Greene St ☎ 941-4777,
Home

Untitled, 4. 159 Prince St ☎ 982-2088,
Art Books/Postcards

Vivienne Tam, 29.
99 Greene St ☎ 966-2398, Clothing

Yohji Yamamoto, 50.
103 Grand St ☎ 966-9066, Clothing

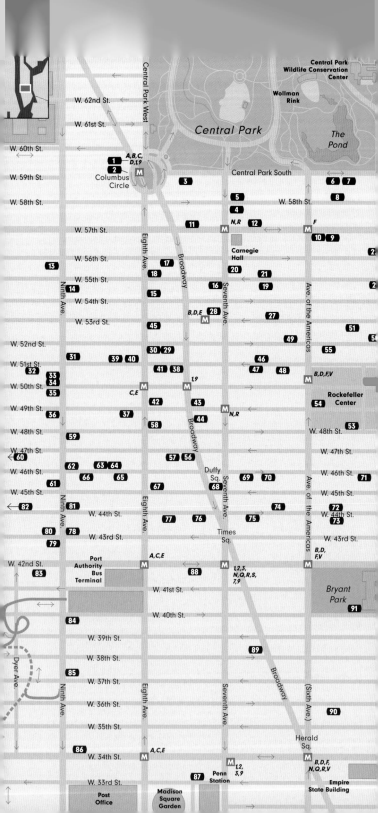

Central Park
Wildlife Conservation
Center

W. 62nd St.

W. 61st St.

Central Park

Wollman
Rink

The
Pond

W. 60th St.

**A,B,C,
D,1,9**

1

2

Columbus
Circle

W. 59th St.

Central Park South

6 **7**

3

8

W. 58th St.

5

W. 58th St.

4

N,R **12**

F

W. 57th St.

11

10 **9**

Carnegie
Hall

W. 56th St.

17

20

2.

18

21

13

W. 55th St.

15

16

19

2.

14

W. 54th St.

Seventh Ave.

W. 53rd St.

B,D,E **28**

27

45

49

51

W. 52nd St.

30 **29**

55

5.

31

39 **40**

46

W. 51st St.

41 **38**

47 **48**

B,D,F,V

32

1,9

33

34

W. 50th St.

C,E

Rockefeller
Center

35

42

43

54

53

W. 49th St.

37

N,R

36

58

44

W. 48th St.

W. 48th St.

59

W. 47th St.

57 **56**

W. 47th St.

60

62

63 **64**

Duffy
Sq.

69 **70**

W. 46th St.

71

66

65

68

W. 46th St.

61

67

Seventh Ave.

W. 45th St.

82

74

72

81

75

73

W. 44th St.

W. 44th St.

80

78

77 **76**

**B,D,
F,V**

79

W. 43rd St.

Times
Sq.

W. 43rd St.

W. 42nd St.

Port
Authority
Bus
Terminal

A,C,E

83

88

**1,2,3,
N,Q,R,S,
7,9**

Bryant
Park

W. 41st St.

W. 40th St.

91

84

W. 39th St.

W. 38th St.

89

85

W. 37th St.

Broadway

W. 36th St.

90

W. 35th St.

Herald
Sq.

86

W. 34th St.

A,C,E

**B,D,F,
N,Q,R,V**

W. 33rd St.

87

**1,2,
3,9**

Penn
Station

Empire
State Building

Post
Office

Madison
Square
Garden

Central Park West

Eighth Ave.

Ninth Ave.

Broadway

Seventh Ave.

Ave. of the Americas

Ave. of the Americas

(Sixth Ave.)

Eighth Ave.

Ninth Ave.

Dyer Ave.

Listed by Site Number

Above, 88. 234 W 42nd St
☎ 642-2626. American. $$$

Acqua Pazza, 55. 36 W 52nd St
☎ 582-6900. Italian Seafood. $$-$$$$

Alain Ducasse NY, 5. 155 W 58th St
☎ 265-7300. French. $$$$

Aquavit, 26. 65 E 55th St
☎ 307-7311. Scandinavian. $$$$

Avra, 128. 141 E 48th St ☎ 759-8550.
Greek Seafood. $$-$$$

Asiate, 1. 80 Columbus Circle
☎ 805-8881. Japanese/French. $$$$

Azalea, 41. 224 W 51st St
☎ 262-0105. Italian. $$-$$$

Baldoria, 42. 249 W 49th St
☎ 582-0460. Italian. $$-$$$

Barbetta, 63. 321 W 46th St
☎ 246-9171. Italian. $$-$$$

Beacon, 22. 25 W 56th St
☎ 332-0500. American. $$-$$$

Becco, 64. 355 W 46th St
☎ 397-7597. Italian. $-$$$

Bellini, 110. 208 E 52nd St
☎ 308-0830. Italian. $$-$$$

Ben Benson's, 49. 123 W 52nd St
☎ 581-8888. Steak. $-$$$

Bienvenue, 119. 21 E 36th St.
☎ 684-0215. French. $-$$

Blue Fin, 56. 1567 Broadway
☎ 918-1400. Seafood. $$-$$$$

Brasserie, 115. 100 E 53rd St
☎ 751-4840. French. $-$$$

Brasserie LCB, 23. 60 W 55th St
☎ 688-6525. French. $$$$

Bryant Park Cafe, 91. 25 W 40th St
☎ 840-6500. American. $-$$

Bryant Park Grill, 91. 25 W 40th St
☎ 840-6500. American. $$-$$$

Cafe Atlas, 7. 40 Central Park S
☎ 759-9191. Contemporary. $$-$$$

Café Gray, 2. 10 Columbus Circle
☎ 823-6338. Eclectic $$$$

Café Un Deux Trois, 74. 123 W 44th St
☎ 354-4148. French. $-$$

Carmine's, 76. 200 W 44th St
☎ 221-3800. Italian. $-$$$$

Carnegie Deli, 16. 854 Seventh Ave
☎ 757-2245. Deli. ¢-$$

Chez Josephine, 83. 414 W 42nd St
☎ 594-1925. International. $$

Chimichurri Grill, 78. 606 Ninth
Ave ☎ 586-8655. Argentine. $-$$

Chin Chin, 125. 216 E 49th St
☎ 888-4555. Chinese. $$-$$$

China Grill, 51. 60 W 53rd St
☎ 333-7788. Pan-Asian. $$

Chola, 95. 232 E 58th St
☎ 688-4619. Indian. $-$$

Churrascaria Plataforma, 37.
316 W 49th St ☎ 245-0505.
Brazilian. $$$$

Cité, 48. 120 W 51st St
☎ 956-7100. Steak. $$-$$$

Columbus Bakery, 108. 957 First Ave
☎ 421-0334. Light Fare. ¢

Cupcake Cafe, 84. 522 Ninth Ave
☎ 465-1530. Bakery/Cafe. ¢

Dawat, 93. 210 E 58th St
☎ 355-7555. Indian. $-$$

db bistro moderne, 73. 55 W 44th St
☎ 391-5353. French. $$$

Delta Grill, 59. 700 Ninth Ave
☎ 956-0934. Cajun. $-$$

District, 70. 130 W 46th St
☎ 485-2999. American. $$-$$$$

Divane, 45. 888 Eighth Ave
☎ 333-5888. Turkish. $

Esca, 79. 402 W 43rd St ☎ 564-7272.
Italian Seafood. $$-$$$

Estiatorio Milos, 21. 125 W 55th St
☎ 245-7400. Greek Seafood.
$$-$$$$

Felidia, 94. 243 E 58th St ☎ 758-1479.
Italian. $-$$$$

5757, 100. 57 E 57th St ☎ 758-5757.
Contemporary. $$-$$$$

Firebird, 62. 365 W 46th St
☎ 586-0244. Russian. $$$-$$$$

Fives, 25. 700 Fifth Ave
☎ 903-3918. Eclectic. $$$-$$$$

Fontana di Trevi, 12. 151 W 57th St
☎ 247-5683. Italian. $-$$

44 & X Hell's Kitchen, 82.
622 Tenth Ave ☎ 977-1170.
American. $$

Four Seasons, 118. 99 E 52nd St
☎ 754-9494. American. $$$-$$$$

Frankie & Johnnie's, 67.
269 W 45th St ☎ 997-9494. Steak.
$$-$$$

$$$$ = over $35 $$$ = $28-$35 $$ = $19-$27 $ = $11-$18   ¢ = under $10
Based on cost per person for an entrée.

Listed Alphabetically (cont.)

Gallagher's, 29. 228 W 52nd St
☎ 245-5336. Steakhouse.
$$-$$$

Grand Sichuan International, 34. 745 Ninth Ave ☎ 582-2288. Chinese. ¢-$

Gustavino's, 96. 409 E 59th St
☎ 980-2455. Eclectic. $-$$$

Hallo Berlin, 32. 402 W 51st St
☎ 541-6248. German. ¢-$

Hard Rock Cafe, 11. 221 W 57th St
☎ 489-6565. American. $

Hatsuhana, 129. 17 E 48th St
☎ 355-3345. Japanese. $$-$$$$

Heartbeat, 127. 149 E 49th St ☎ 407-2900. Contemporary. $$-$$$

Houston's, 113. 153 E 53rd St
☎ 888-3828. American. $-$$

Ida Mae, 89. 111 W 38th St
☎ 704-0038. New American. $-$$

Inagiku, 120. 111 E 49th St
☎ 355-0440. Japanese. $$$-$$$$

Island Burgers & Shakes, 31.
766 Ninth Ave ☎ 307-7934. ¢

John's Pizzeria, 77. 260 W 44th St
☎ 391-7560. Pizza. ¢-$

Josephs, 54. 1240 Sixth Ave
☎ 332-1515. Seafood. $$-$$$$

Josie's, 142. 565 Third Ave
☎ 490-1558. Healthy. $-$$

Keen's, 90. 72 W 36th St ☎ 947-3636. Steak. $$-$$$

Kuruma Zushi, 132. 7 E 47th St
☎ 317-2802. Japanese. $$-$$$$

La Grenouille, 117. 3 E 52nd St
☎ 752-1495. French. $$$-$$$$

La Locanda, 37. 737 Ninth Ave
☎ 258-2900. Italian. $-$$

Le Bernardin, 46. 155 W 51st St
☎ 489-1515. French Seafood. $$$$

Le Colonial, 95. 149 E 57th St
☎ 752-0808. Vietnamese. $-$$

Le Madeleine, 76. 403 W 43rd St
☎ 246-2993. French. $-$$

Le Marais, 65. 150 W 46th St
☎ 869-0900. French/Kosher. $$-$$$

Le Perigord, 109. 405 E 52nd St
☎ 755-6244. French. $$$$

Le Rivage, 66. 340 W 46th St
☎ 765-7374. French. $$$

Lever House, 104. 390 Park Ave
☎ 888-2700. Contemporary. $$-$$$$

L'Impero, 140. 45 Tudor City Pl
☎ 599-5045. Italian. $$-$$$

Maloney & Porcelli, 117. 37 E 50th St
☎ 750-2233. Contemporary. $$-$$$

Mangia, 9. 50 W 57th St
☎ 582-5882. Italian. ¢-$

Manhattan Ocean Club, 8.
57 W 58th St ☎ 371-7777. Seafood.
$$-$$$

March, 97. 405 E 58th St ☎ 754-6272.
Contemporary. $$$$

Marichu, 138. 342 E 46th St
☎ 370-1866. Spanish. $-$$

Market Cafe, 85. 496 Ninth Ave
☎ 564-7350. American. ¢-$

Mars 2112, 38. 1633 Broadway
☎ 582-2112. Eclectic. $-$$

Marseille, 81. 630 Ninth Ave
☎ 333-3410. French. $$

Masa, 2. 10 Columbus Circle
☎ 823-9800. Japanese. $$$$

Meskerem, 60. 468 W 47th St
☎ 664-0520. Ethiopian. ¢-$

Michael Jordan's The Steak House NYC, 132. 23 Vanderbilt Ave
☎ 655-2300. Steak. $$$-$$$$

Mickey Mantle's, 6. 42 Central Park S
☎ 688-7777. American. $-$$

Molyvos, 20. 871 Seventh Ave
☎ 582-7500. Greek. $$-$$$

Montparnasse, 121. 230 E 51st St
☎ 758-6633. French. $$

Morton's, 131. 551 Fifth Ave
☎ 972-3315. Steak. $$$$

Nanni's, 134. 146 E 46th St
☎ 697-4161. Italian. $$-$$$

Nick & Stef's Steakhouse, 87.
9 Penn Plaza ☎ 563-4444.
Steak. $$-$$$

Nippon, 111. 155 E 52nd St
☎ 758-0226. Japanese. $$-$$$

Nocello, 18. 257 W 55th St
☎ 713-0224. Italian. $-$$

Noche, 44. 1604 Broadway
☎ 541-7070. Latin. $$

Oceana, 101. 55 E 54th St
☎ 759-5941. Seafood. $$$$

Ola, 126. 304 E 48th St
☎ 759-0590. Pan-Latin. $-$$$

Orso, 65. 322 W 46th St ☎ 489-7212.
Italian. $$

Osteria del Circo, 19. 120 W 55th St
☎ 265-3636. Italian. $$-$$$

Oyster Bar, 133. Grand Central Terminal
☎ 490-6650. Seafood. $$-$$$

Palm, 137. 837 Second Ave
☎ 687-2953. Steak. $-$$$$

Pampano, 124. 209 E 49th St
☎ 751-4545. Mexican. $$

Pam Real Thai, 36. 404 W 49th St
☎ 333-7500. Thai. ¢-$

Patroon, 135. 160 E 46th St
☎ 883-7373. American. $$-$$$$

Patsy's, 17. 236 W 56th St
☎ 247-3491. Italian. $$-$$$

Peking Duck, 107. 236 E 53rd St
☎ 759-8260. Chinese. $-$$

Per Se, 2. 10 Columbus Circle
☎ 823-9335. French. $$$$

Petrossian, 4. 182 W 58th St
☎ 245-2214. Continental. $$-$$$$

Pierre au Tunnel, 57. 250 W 47th St
☎ 575-1220. French. $$-$$$

Pigalle, 58. 790 Eighth Ave
☎ 489-2233. French. ¢-$$

Planet Hollywood, 68.
1540 Broadway ☎ 333-7827.
American. $-$$

Puttanesca, 13. 859 Ninth Ave
☎ 581-4177. Italian. $

Red Garlic, 15. 916 8th Ave
☎ 489-5237. Thai. ¢-$

Remi, 27. 145 W 53rd St ☎ 581-4242.
Italian. $$-$$$

René Pujol, 39. 321 W 51st St
☎ 246-3023. French. $$-$$$

Rosa Mexicano, 98. 1063 First Ave
☎ 753-7407. Mexican. $-$$$

Ruby Foo's, 43. 1626 Broadway
☎ 489-5600. Pan-Asian. $-$$

Rue 57, 10. 60 W 57th St
☎ 307-5656. French/Japanese. $$

Ruth's Chris Steakhouse, 47.
148 W 51st St ☎ 245-9600.
Steak. $$$-$$$$

San Domenico, 3. 240 Central Park S
☎ 265-5959. Italian. $$-$$$$

San Pietro, 102. 18 E 54th St
☎ 753-9015. Italian. $$-$$$

Sea Grill, 52. 19 W 49th St
☎ 332-7610. Seafood. $$-$$$

Shaan, 53. Rockefeller Ctr, 57 W 48th St
☎ 977-8400. Indian. $-$$

Shun Lee Palace, 105.
155 E 55th St ☎ 371-8844.
Chinese. $$$$

Smith & Wollensky, 123.
797 Third Ave ☎ 753-1530.
Steak. $$-$$$$

Solera, 106. 216 E 53rd St
☎ 644-1166. Spanish. $$$-$$$$

Soul Fixins', 86. 371 W 34th St
☎ 736-1345. Soul. ¢-$

Sparks Steak House, 136.
210 E 46th St ☎ 687-4855. Steak.
$$-$$$$

Stage Deli, 28. 834 Seventh Ave
☎ 245-7850. Deli. ¢-$

Sushi Yasuda, 139. 204 E 43rd St
☎ 972-1001. Japanese. $-$$$

Sushiden, 118. 19 E 49th St
☎ 758-2700. Japanese. $$-$$$

Tao, 92. 42 E 58th St ☎ 888-2288.
Pan-Asian. $$-$$$$

Tout Va Bien, 40. 311 W 51st St
☎ 265-0190. French. $-$$

Town, 24. 15 W 56th St ☎ 582-4445.
Contemporary. $$$

Trio, 143. 167 E 33rd St
☎ 685-1001. Italian. $$

Triomphe, 72. 49 W 44th St
☎ 453-4233. French. $$-$$$

Tse Yang, 116. 34 E 51st St
☎ 688-5447. Chinese. $$-$$$$

21 Club, 50. 21 W 52nd St
☎ 582-7200. American. $$$-$$$$

Uncle Nick's, 33. 747 Ninth Ave
☎ 245-7992. Greek. $

Via Brasil, 71. 34 W 46th St
☎ 997-1158. Brazilian. $

Victor's Café, 30. 236 W 52nd St
☎ 586-7714. Cuban. $-$$$

Virgil's Real BBQ, 75. 152 W 44th St
☎ 921-9494. Barbecue. $-$$

V Steakhouse, 2. 10 Columbus Ave
☎ 823-9500. Steak. $$-$$$$

Vong, 112. 200 E 54th St ☎ 486-9592.
Pan-Asian. $-$$$$

Vynl, 14. 824 Ninth Ave ☎ 974-2003.
Eclectic. ¢-$$

Wu Liang Ye, 141. 338 Lexington Ave
☎ 370-9647. Chinese. ¢-$$

Zarela, 122. 953 Second Ave
☎ 644-6740. Mexican. $

Zen Palate, 61. 663 Ninth Ave
☎ 582-1669. Vegetarian. ¢-$

$$$$ = *over $35* $$$ = *$28-$35* $$ = *$19-$27* $ = *$11-$18*   ¢ = *under $10*
Based on cost per person for an entrée.

Listed by Site Number

1	Charles's	18	Artie's Delicatessen	35	Citrus
2	Sylvia's	19	Fred's	36	Josie's
3	Bayou	20	Columbus Bakery	37	Shark Bar
4	Terrace	21	Rain	38	Penang
5	Pampa	22	Calle Ocho	39	Pasha
6	Gabriela's	23	EJ's Luncheonette	40	Café Luxembourg
7	Gennaro	24	Haru	41	Café des Artistes
8	Saigon Grill	25	Cafe con Leche	42	Tavern on the Green
9	Docks	26	Sarabeth's	43	Shun Lee West
10	AIX	27	La Grolla	44	Ollie's
11	Carmine's	28	Nice Matin	45	Picholine
12	Alouette	29	Ocean Grill	46	Cafe Fiorello
13	Barney Greengrass	30	Sushi of Gari	46	Josephina
14	Nonna	31	Cafe Frida	47	Gabriel's
15	Edgar's Cafe	32	Ruby Foo's	48	Jean Georges
16	Ouest	33	Isabella's	49	Conservatory Cafe
17	Good Enough to Eat	34	'Cesca	50	Rosa Mexicano

$$$$ = *over $35* $$$ = *$28-$35* $$ = *$19-$27* $ = *$11-$18*   ¢ = *under $10*
Based on cost per person for an entrée.

Listed by Site Number

Atlantic Grill, 19. 1341 Third Ave
☎ 988–9200. Seafood. $–$$

Aureole, 46. 34 E 61st St ☎ 319–1660.
Contemporary. $$$$

Café Boulud, 17. 20 E 76th St
☎ 772–2600. French. $$–$$$

Café Sabarsky, 1. 1048 Fifth Ave
☎ 288–0665. Austrian. $–$$

Caffè Bianco, 21. 1486 Second Ave
☎ 988–2655. Light Fare. ¢–$

Candle Cafe, 31. 1307 Third Ave
☎ 472–0970. Vegetarian. ¢–$$

Canyon Road, 24. 1470 First Ave
☎ 734–1600. Southwestern. $$

Centolire, 4. 1167 Madison Ave
☎ 734–7711. Italian. $–$$$

Circus, 44. 808 Lexington Ave
☎ 223–2965. Brazilian. $$–$$$

Daniel, 41. 60 E 65th St ☎ 288–0033.
French. $$$$

Dumonet, 16. Carlyle Hotel, 35 E 76th St
☎ 744–1600. French. $$$–$$$$

E.A.T., 12. 1064 Madison Ave
☎ 772–0022. Light Fare. $–$$

Etats-Unis, 10. 242 E 81st St
☎ 517–8826. Eclectic. $$–$$$

Ikeno Hana, 32. 1016 Lexington Ave
☎ 737–6639. Japanese. $–$$

JG Melon, 29. 1291 Third Ave
☎ 744–0585. American. ¢–$

Jo Jo, 40. 160 E 64th St ☎ 223–5656.
French. $–$$$

Kai, 36. 822 Madison Ave
☎ 988–7277. Japanese. $$$$

Lenox, 33. 1278 Third Ave ☎ 772–0404.
American $$–$$$

Luca, 6. 1712 First Ave ☎ 987–9260.
Italian. $–$$

Lusardi's, 22. 1494 Second Ave
☎ 249–2020. Italian. $$

Manhattan Grille, 38. 1161 First Ave
☎ 888–6556. Steak. $$–$$$$

Mark's Restaurant, 14. 25 E 77th St
☎ 879–1864. Continental. $$$–$$$$

Maya, 37. 1191 First Ave ☎ 585–1818.
Mexican. $$

Mezzaluna, 30. 1295 Third Ave
☎ 535–9600. Italian. $–$$

Mocca, 8. 1588 Second Ave
☎ 734–6470. Hungarian. $

Nicole's, 47. 10 E 60th St
☎ 223–2288. Contemporary.
$$$

Orsay, 18. 1057-1059 Lexington
Ave ☎ 517–6400. French. $$–$$$$

Pamir, 26. 1437 Second Ave
☎ 734–3791. Afghan. $

Park Avenue Café, 43. 100 E 63rd St
☎ 644–1900. American. $$–$$$

Payard Patisserie & Bistro, 28.
1032 Lexington Ave ☎ 717–5252.
French. $$–$$$$

Persepolis, 27. 1423 Second Ave
☎ 535–1100. Persian. $

Pio Pio, 7. 1746 First Ave ☎ 426–5800.
Peruvian. ¢–$

Post House, 42. 28 E 63rd St
☎ 935–2888. Steak. $$$–$$$$

Rain, 39. 1059 Third Ave
☎ 223–3669. Pan-Asian. $

rm, 48. 33 E 60th St ☎ 319–3800.
Seafood. $$$$

Saigon Grill, 5. 1700 Second Ave
☎ 996–4600. Vietnamese. ¢–$

Sarabeth's, 3. 1295 Madison Ave
☎ 410–7335. American. $–$$

Serafina Fabulous Pizza, 13.
1022 Madison Ave ☎ 734–2676.
Pizza. ¢–$$

Serendipity 3, 45. 225 E 60th St
☎ 838–3531. American. $–$$

Sistina, 9. 1555 Second Ave
☎ 861–7660. Italian. $$–$$$

Sushi of Gari, 25. 402 E 78th St
☎ 517–5340. Japanese. $–$$$$

Table d'Hote, 2. 44 E 92nd St
☎ 348–8125. French. $$

Taperia Madrid, 20. 1471 Second Ave
☎ 794–2923. Tapas. $$$

Toraya, 34. 17 E 71st St
☎ 861–1700. Japanese. ¢–$

Trata, 35. 1331 Second Ave
☎ 535–3800. Greek. $–$$

Vermicelli, 23. 1492 Second Ave
☎ 288–8868. Vietnamese. ¢–$

Viand, 15. 1011 Madison Ave
☎ 249–8250. Coffee Shop. ¢–$

Zócalo, 11. 174 E 82nd St ☎ 717–7772.
Mexican. $$

$$$$ = *over $35* $$$ = *$28–$35* $$ = *$19–$27* $ = *$11–$18*   ¢ = *under $10*
Based on cost per person for an entrée.

MAP 49 Restaurants/Chelsea, Flatiron District

Listed by Site Number

Listed by Site Number

Listed Alphabetically

Amuse, 53. 108 W 18th St
☎ 929-9755. Eclectic. $-$$$$

Arezzo, 49. 46 W 22nd St
☎ 206-0555. Italian. $$-$$$

Artisanal, 5. 2 Park Ave ☎ 725-8585.
French. $-$$$$

Bao Noodles, 21. 391 Second Ave
☎ 725-7770. Vietnamese. ¢-$$

Barking Dog, 6. 150 E 34th St
☎ 871-3900. American. ¢-$

The Basil, 59. 206 W 23rd St
☎ 242-1014. Thai. $-$$

Beppe, 23. 45 E 22nd St ☎ 982-8422.
Italian. $-$$$$

Biltmore Room, 62. 290 Eighth Ave
☎ 807-0111. Asian Fusion. $$-$$$

Biricchino, 58. 260 W 29th St
☎ 695-6690. Italian. $-$$

Blue Smoke, 17. 116 E 27th St
☎ 447-7733. Barbecue. ¢-$$

Blue Water Grill, 38. 31 Union Sq W
☎ 675-9500. Seafood. $-$$$

Bolo, 47. 23 E 22nd St ☎ 228-2200.
Spanish. $$-$$$

Bongo, 82. 299 Tenth Ave
☎ 947-3694. Seafood. $$

Bottino, 83. 246 Tenth Ave
☎ 206-6766. Italian. $$-$$$

Bread Bar, 19. 11 Madison Ave
☎ 889-0667. Indian. $-$$

Bright Food Shop, 65.
216 Eighth Ave ☎ 243-4433.
Eclectic. $$

Cafe Riazor, 83. 245 W 16th St
☎ 727-2132. Spanish. $-$$

Cafeteria, 56. 119 Seventh Ave
☎ 414-1717. American. $-$$

Casa Mono, 33. 52 Irving Pl
☎ 253-2773. Tapas. ¢-$

Caviar and Banana, 46. 12 E 22nd St
☎ 353-0300. Brazilian. $-$$$

Chelsea Bistro, 79. 358 W 23rd St
☎ 727-2026. French. $$$

Chennai Garden, 15.
129 E 27th St ☎ 689-1999.
Indian/Vegetarian. ¢-$

City Bakery, 52. 3 W 18th St
☎ 366-1414. Cafe/Bakery. ¢-$

Craft, 30. 49 E 19th St ☎ 780-0880.
New American. $$-$$$$

Craftbar, 29. 47 E 19th St
☎ 780-0880. Italian. $-$$

Curry Leaf, 14. 99 Lexington Ave
☎ 725-5558. Indian. ¢-$$$

Da Umberto, 54. 107 W 17th St
☎ 989-0303. Italian. $$

Dévi, 44. 8 E 18th St
☎ 691-1300. Indian. $$$

Don Giovanni, 88. 214 Tenth Ave
☎ 242-9054. Italian/Pizza. ¢

Dos Caminos, 18. 373 Park Ave S
☎ 294-1000. Mexican. $-$$

Duvet, 50. 45 W 18th St
☎ 989-2121. American. $$$

Eisenberg's Sandwich Shop, 48.
174 Fifth Ave ☎ 675-5096.
American. ¢

Eleven Madison Park, 19.
11 Madison Ave ☎ 889-0905.
Contemporary. $$-$$$

Elmo, 57. 156 Seventh Ave
☎ 337-8000. American. $

F & B, 57. 269 W 23rd St
☎ 646/486-4441. Hotdogs. ¢

Fleur de Sel, 45. 5 E 20th St
☎ 460-9100. French. $$$-$$$$

Frank's, 90. 85 Tenth Ave
☎ 243-1349. Steakhouse. $$$

Gam Mee Ok, 1. 43 W 32nd St
☎ 695-4113. Korean. ¢-$$

Gascogne, 68. 158 Eighth Ave
☎ 675-6564. French. $$

Gramercy Tavern, 27. 42 E 20th St
☎ 477-0777. American. $$$$

Grand Sichuan, 81. 229 Ninth Ave
☎ 620-5200. Chinese. ¢-$

Green Table, 73. 75 Ninth Ave
☎ 741-6623. New American. ¢-$

Half King, 85. 505 W 23rd St
☎ 462-4300. Irish. ¢-$

Hangawi, 4. 12 E 32nd St
☎ 213-0077. Korean/Vegetarian.
$-$$$$

Havana Central, 41. 22 E 17th St
☎ 414-2298. Cuban. ¢-$

Havana Chelsea, 67. 190 Eighth Ave
☎ 243-9421. Cuban. ¢-$

I Trulli, 16. 122 E 27th St
☎ 481-7372. Italian. $$-$$$

Kang Suh, 2. 32 W 32nd St
☎ 947-8482. Korean. ¢-$$

Kitchen 22, 24. 36 E 22nd St
☎ 228-4399. American. $$

La Bergamote, 78. 169 Ninth Ave
☎ 627-9010. Bakery/Cafe. ¢

La Bottega, 83. 88 Ninth Ave
☎ 243-8400. Italian. $

La Lunchonette, 67. 130 Tenth Ave
☎ 675-0342. French. $-$$

La Taza de Oro, 72. 96 Eighth Ave
☎ 243-9946. Puerto Rican. ¢

Le Pain Quotidien, 31. 38 E 19th St
☎ 673-7900. Bakery/Cafe. ¢

Les Halles, 8. 411 Park Ave S
☎ 679-4111. French. $-$$

Le Zie, 58. 172 Seventh Ave
☎ 206-8686. Italian. $

Los Dos Molinos, 32. 119 E 18th St
☎ 505-1574. Mexican. $-$$

Lucy, 35. 35 E 18th St
☎ 475-5829. Mexican. ¢-$$

Mad 28, 20. 72 Madison Ave
☎ 689-2828. Italian/Pizza. $

Mandoo Bar, 3. 2 W 32nd St
☎ 279-3075. Korean. ¢-$

Marchi's, 9. 251 E 31st St
☎ 679-2494. Italian. $$$$

Maroons, 55. 244 W 16th St
☎ 206-8640. Caribbean. $

Matsuri, 74. 363 W 16th St
☎ 243-6400. Japanese. $-$$

Mesa Grill, 43. 102 Fifth Ave
☎ 807-7400. Southwestern. $$-$$$

Negril, 80. 362 W 23rd St
☎ 807-6411. Jamaican. ¢-$$

Novitá, 22. 102 E 22nd St
☎ 677-2222. Italian. $

Olives NY, 37. 201 Park Ave S
☎ 353-8345. Italian. $$-$$$

O Mai, 77. 158 Ninth Ave
☎ 633-0550. Vietnamese $

The Park, 89. 118 Tenth Ave
☎ 352-3313. New American. $

Park Bistro, 7. 414 Park Ave S
☎ 689-1360. French. $$-$$$

Patria, 28. 250 Park Ave S
☎ 777-6211. Latin. $$-$$$

Periyali, 51. 35 W 20th St
☎ 463-7890. Greek. $$

Pipa, 31. 38 E 19th St ☎ 677-2233.
Spanish. $-$$

Pongal, 12. 110 Lexington Ave
☎ 696-9458. Indian/Vegetarian. ¢-$

Pop Burger, 83. 58-60 Ninth Ave
☎ 414-8686. American. ¢

The Red Cat, 84. 227 Tenth Ave
☎ 242-1122. American. $$

Republic, 40. 37A Union Sq W
☎ 627-7172. Pan-Asian. ¢-$

Rocking Horse Cafe, 66. 182 Eighth
Ave ☎ 463-9511. Mexican. $-$$

Seven, 60. 350 Seventh Ave
☎ 967-1919. American. $$

Sueños, 69. 311 W 17th St
☎ 243-1333. Mexican. $-$$

Tabla, 19. 11 Madison Ave
☎ 889-0667. Indian Fusion. $$$-$$$$

Tamarind, 25. 41-43 E 22nd St
☎ 674-7400. Indian. $-$$$

Tia Pol, 86. 205 Tenth Ave
☎ 675-8805. Tapas. $

Toqueville, 42. 15 E 15th St
☎ 647-1515. New American.
$$$-$$$$

Trailer Park, 63. 271 W 23rd St
☎ 463-8000. American. ¢

Turkish Kitchen, 13. 386 Third Ave
☎ 679-1810. Turkish. $-$$

Union Square Café, 39. 21 E 16th St
☎ 243-4020. American. $$-$$$

Vatan, 11. 409 Third Ave
☎ 689-5666. Indian/Vegetarian. $$

Veritas, 26. 43 E 20th St ☎ 353-3700.
Contemporary. $$$$

Water Club, 10. 500 E 30th St
☎ 683-3333. Seafood. $$$-$$$$

Wild Lily Tea Room, 87.
511-A W 22nd St ☎ 691-2258.
Eclectic/Tea House. ¢-$

Yama, 34. 122 E 17th St ☎ 475-0969.
Japanese. $-$$

Zen Palate, 36. 34 Union Sq E
☎ 614-9291. Vegetarian/Asian. ¢

$$$$ = *over $35* $$$ = *$28-$35* $$ = *$19-$27* $ = *$11-$18*   ¢ = *under $10*
Based on cost per person for an entrée.

Union Square Park

A,C,E,L 1,2,3,9 F,L,V

2
3
4
5

1

6
7
8

9

L,N,R,
4,5,6

W. 14th St.
W. 13th St.
W. 12th St.
W. 11th St.
W. 10th St.
W. 9th St.

Fifth Ave.

University Pl.

10 **11** **12**

13

30

Little
W. 12th St.

Gansevoort St.
Horatio St.
Jane St.
W. 12th St.
Bethune St.
Bank St.

Greenwich St.

Abingdon
Square

17

18

19

Eighth Ave.

W. 4th St.

Seventh
Ave. S.

Greenwich Ave.

Perry St.
Charles St.
W. 10th St.

16
15
20

21
23
24
22

Grove St.
Commerce St.

Milligan Pl.
Patchin Pl.

Gay St.

Waverly Pl.

Christopher St.

Sheridan
Square

27
29
25

28

W. 8th St.

MacDougal
Alley

Washington
Mews

Waverly Pl.

Washington Sq. N.

W. Washington Pl.

Washington Sq. S.

*Washington
Square Park*

E. Washington
Pl.

New York University

W. 3rd St.

A,C,
E,F,V

31
33

32

34 **36**
35

42

37

St. Luke's
Pl.

Barrow St.
Morton St.
Leroy St.
Clarkson St.
W. Houston St.

King St.
Charlton St.
Vandam St.

Washington St.

Hudson St.

Bleecker St.
Bedford St.
Carmine St.
Downing St.

*GREENWICH
VILLAGE*

38

39
40
41

43

44

45

46
47

48

49

Minetta La.
Father
Demo Sq.

Bleecker St.

W. Houston St.

B,D,F,V

50
51 **52**

53

54 **55**

Sullivan St.
Thompson St.
MacDougal St.
Ave. of the Americas

LaGuardia Pl.

West Broadway

Wooster St.
Greene St.
Mercer St.
Broadway

C,E
(Sixth Ave.)

109

108

Grand St.

Spring St.
Dominick St.

Broome

Holland Tunnel
Entrance

*Hudson
River
Park*

West St.

West Side Highway

Watts St.
Desbrosses St.
Vestry St.
Laight St.
Hubert St.

Greenwich St.

110

Holland
Tunnel
Exit

A,C,E
1,9
Canal St.

R,Q,W

Church St.

Lispenard St.

Walker St.

Greene St.
Broadway

White
St.

Holland Tunnel

Hudson River

N

1200 feet

400 meters

Beach St.

Ericsson
Pl.

Varick St.

111

114
115
116
118 **117**

N. Moore St.
Franklin St.

**Manhattan
Community College**

Jay St.
Staple St.

Harrison St.

Independence
Plaza

119

Chambers St.

Warren St.
Park Pl.
Murray St.

North End Ave.

River Terrace

West St.

112

113

Leonard St.
Worth St.

126
125 **127** **129**
124 **128** **123**
122

120 **121**

Franklin St.
Catherine

Thomas St.
Duane St.
Reade St.

1,2,3,9

A,C

Warren St.
Murray St.

2,3

R,W

City
Hall
Park

Washington St.

Chambers St.

Greenwich St.

Park Pl.
Barclay St.
Vesey St.

R,W

Church St.

C,E

A,C

Hudson River

Vesey St.

**World Trade
Center
Site**

Fulton St.

4,5,6

Dey St.

4,5

Cortlandt St.

N,R

**World
Financial
Center**

West St.

West Side Highway

South End Ave.

Liberty St.
1,9 (Closed)

Cedar St.
Albany St.
Carlisle

141

Albany

143

**BATTERY
PARK
CITY**

Liberty St.

Cedar St.
Thames
St.

142

Washington St.
Greenwich St.

Trinity Pl.

4,5 Wall St.

Exchange Pl.

Rector St.
1,9

Listed by Site Number

1 Crispo
2 Spice Market
3 Pastis
4 Florent
5 Macelleria
6 Café de Bruxelles
7 Benny's Burritos
8 Good
9 Café Loup
10 Strip House
11 Japonica
12 Gotham Bar & Grill
13 Cafe Spice
14 Jefferson
15 La Metairie
16 Mary's Fish Camp
17 Jarnac
18 Philip Marie
19 Wallsé
20 August
21 Surya
22 Pink Tea Cup
23 One If By Land, Two If By Sea
24 Annisa
25 Home
26 Pó
27 Pearl Oyster Bar
28 Babbo
29 Blue Hill
30 Cru
31 John's Pizzeria
32 Petite Abeille
33 Snack Taverna
34 Do Hwa
35 Deborah
36 Blue Ribbon Bakery
37 'Ino
38 Villa Mosconi
39 Lupa
40 Tomoe Sushi
41 Arturo's
42 Brothers Bar-B-Q
43 Provence
44 Jean Claude
45 Raoul's
46 Blue Ribbon
47 Mezzogiorno
48 Aquagrill
49 Blue Ribbon Sushi

50 Honmura An
51 Woo Lae Oak
52 Canteen
53 Mercer Kitchen
54 Fanelli's
55 Zoë
56 Balthazar
57 Moustache
58 Gnocco
59 Bao 111
60 I Coppi
61 La Palapa
62 Second Ave Deli
63 Danal
64 Hasaki
65 La Paella
66 Otafuku
67 Holy Basil
68 Angelica Kitchen
69 Rai Rai Ken
70 Veselka
71 Mingala
72 Dok Suni's
73 Miracle Grill
74 Raga
75 Takahachi
76 Le Souk
77 First
78 Haveli
79 Jewel Bako
80 Great Jones Cafe
81 Il Buco
82 Acme Bar & Grill
83 Bond Street
84 Five Points
85 Prune
86 Tasting Room
87 Il Bagatto
88 Chubo
89 Paladar
90 Katz's Delicatessen
91 Rialto
92 Ghenet
93 Savoy
94 Spring Street Natural
95 Café Habana
96 Eight Mile Creek
97 Porcupine
98 71 Clinton Fresh Food
99 'inoteca

100 Alias
101 Bar Tonno
102 Bread
103 Sammy's Roumanian
104 Rice
105 Le Jardin
106 Lombardi's
107 Nyonya
108 Cendrillon
109 Pfiff
110 Dylan Prime
111 Montrachet
112 Arqua
113 Layla
114 Bubby's
115 Nobu
116 Tribeca Grill
117 Chanterelle
118 The Harrison
119 Salaam Bombay
120 Kitchenette
121 Ecco
122 Nam
123 Fresh
124 Danube
125 Duane Park Café
126 Odeon
127 City Hall
128 Bouley
129 Megu
130 Thailand
131 Jing Fong
132 Great New York Noodletown
133 Joe's Shanghai
134 Sweet 'n' Tart
135 Ping's Seafood
136 New Indonesia & Malaysia
137 Canton
138 Dim Sum Go Go
139 Bridge Café
140 Les Halles
141 Roy's New York
142 14 Wall Street
143 2 West
144 Bayard's

Acme Bar & Grill, 82. 9 Great Jones St
☎ 420-1934. Southern. ¢-$

Alias, 100. 76 Clinton St
☎ 505-5011. New American. $-$$

Angelica Kitchen, 68. 300 E 12th St
☎ 228-2909. Vegetarian. ¢-$

Annisa, 24. 13 Barrow St ☎ 741-6699.
Contemporary. $$-$$$

Aquagrill, 48. 210 Spring St
☎ 274-0505. Seafood. $$

Arqua, 112. 281 Church St
☎ 334-1888. Italian. $$

Arturo's, 41. 106 W Houston St
☎ 677-3820. Pizza. $-$$$

August, 20. 359 Bleecker St
☎ 929-4774. Eclectic. $$$

Babbo, 28. 110 Waverly Pl
☎ 777-0303. Italian. $$-$$$

Balthazar, 56. 80 Spring St
☎ 965-1414. French. $-$$$

Bao 111, 59. 111 Ave C
☎ 254-7773. Vietnamese. $-$$

Bar Tonno, 101. 17 Cleveland Pl
☎ 966-7334. Italian Seafood. ¢-$

Bayard's, 144. 1 Hanover Sq
☎ 514-9454. French. $$$-$$$$

Benny's Burritos, 7. 113 Greenwich Ave
☎ 727-0584. Mexican. ¢

Blue Hill, 29. 75 Washington Pl
☎ 539-1776. Contemporary. $$

Blue Ribbon, 46. 97 Sullivan St
☎ 274-0404. Eclectic. $-$$$

Blue Ribbon Bakery, 36.
33 Downing St ☎ 337-0404.
American. $-$$$

Blue Ribbon Sushi, 49. 119 Sullivan St
☎ 343-0404. Japanese. $-$$$$

Bond Street, 83. 6 Bond St
☎ 777-2500. Japanese. $$$

Bouley, 128. 120 W Broadway
☎ 964-2525. French. $-$$$$

Bread, 102. 20 Spring St
☎ 334-1015. Italian. ¢-$

Bridge Cafe, 139. 279 Water St
☎ 227-3344. American. $$-$$$

Brothers Bar-B-Q, 42. 225 Varick St
☎ 727-2775. Barbecue. ¢-$

Bubby's, 114. 120 Hudson St
☎ 219-0666. American. $-$$

Café de Bruxelles, 6.
118 Greenwich Ave ☎ 206-1830.
Belgian. $-$$

Café Habana, 95. 17 Prince St
☎ 625-2001. Latin. ¢-$

Cafe Lebowitz, 101. 14 Spring St
☎ 219-2399. Eclectic. ¢-$$

Café Loup, 9. 105 W 13th St
☎ 255-4746. French. $-$$

Cafe Spice, 13. 72 University Pl
☎ 253-6999. Indian. $-$$

Canteen, 52. 142 Mercer St
☎ 431-7676. American. $-$$

Canton, 137. 45 Division St
☎ 226-4441. Chinese. $$

Cendrillon, 108. 45 Mercer St
☎ 343-9012. Philippine. $-$$

Chanterelle, 117. 2 Harrison St
☎ 966-6960. French. $$$$

Chubo, 88. 6 Clinton St
☎ 674-6300. Electic. $-$$

City Hall, 127. 131 Duane St
☎ 227-7777. American. $$-$$$

Crispo, 1. 240 W 14th St
☎ 229-1818. Italian. $

Cru, 30. 24 Fifth Ave
☎ 529-1700. New American. $$$-$$$$

Danal, 63. 90 E 10th St
☎ 982-6930. Eclectic. $$

Danube, 124. 30 Hudson St
☎ 791-3771. Austrian. $$-$$$

Deborah, 35. 43 Carmine St
☎ 242-2606. American. $-$$

Dim Sum Go Go, 138. 5 E Broadway
☎ 732-0797. Chinese. ¢-$

Do Hwa, 34. 55 Carmine St
☎ 414-1224. Korean. $-$$

Dok Suni's, 72. 119 First Ave
☎ 477-9506. Korean. $

Duane Park Café, 125. 157 Duane St
☎ 732-5555. Contemporary. $$$

Dylan Prime, 110. 62 Laight St
☎ 334-2274. Steak. $-$$$$

Ecco, 121. 124 Chambers St
☎ 227-7074. Italian. $$-$$$

Eight Mile Creek, 96. 240 Mulberry St
☎ 431-4635. Australian. $$

Fanelli's, 54. 94 Prince St
☎ 226-9412. American. $

First, 77. 87 First Ave
☎ 674-3823. American. $-$$

$$$$ = *over $35* $$$ = *$28-$35* $$ = *$19-$27* $ = *$11-$18*   ¢ = *under $10*
Based on cost per person for an entrée.

MAP 50 Restaurants/The Village & Downtown

Listed Alphabetically (cont.)

Five Points, 84. 31 Great Jones St
☎ 253-5700. Contemporary. $-$$

Florent, 4. 69 Gansevoort St
☎ 989-5779. French. $-$$

14 Wall Street, 142. 14 Wall St
☎ 233-2780. French. $$$

Fresh, 123. 105 Reade St
☎ 406-1900. Seafood. $$-$$$$

Ghenet, 92. 284 Mulberry St
☎ 343-1888. Ethiopian. ¢-$

Gnocco, 58. 337 E Tenth St
☎ 677-1913. Italian. ¢-$

Good, 8. 89 Greenwich Ave
☎ 691-8080. Eclectic. $-$$

Gotham Bar & Grill, 12. 12 E 12th St
☎ 620-4020. Contemporary.
$$$-$$$$

Great Jones Cafe, 80.
54 Great Jones St ☎ 674-9304.
Cajun. ¢-$

Great New York Noodletown, 132.
28 1/2 Bowery ☎ 349-0923.
Chinese. ¢-$$

The Harrison, 118. 355 Greenwich St
☎ 274-9310. American $$-$$$

Hasaki, 64. 210 E 9th St
☎ 473-3327. Japanese. $-$$

Haveli, 78. 100 Second Ave
☎ 982-0533. Indian. ¢-$$

Holy Basil, 67. 149 Second Ave
☎ 460-5557. Thai. ¢-$

Home, 25. 20 Cornelia St
☎ 243-9579. American. ¢-$$

Honmura An, 50. 170 Mercer St
☎ 334-5253. Japanese. $-$$

I Coppi, 60. 432 E 9th St
☎ 254-2263. Italian. $-$$

Il Bagatto, 87. 192 E 2nd St
☎ 228-0977. Italian. $

Il Buco, 81. 47 Bond St
☎ 533-1932. Italian. $$-$$$

'Ino, 37. 21 Bedford St
☎ 989-5769. Italian. ¢

'inoteca, 99. 98 Rivington St
☎ 614-0473. Italian. ¢-$

Japonica, 11. 100 University Pl
☎ 243-7752. Japanese. $$$

Jarnac, 17. 328 W 12th St
☎ 924-3413. French. $$

Jean Claude, 44. 137 Sullivan St
☎ 475-9232. French. $$

Jefferson, 14. 121 W 10th St
☎ 255-3333. New American. $-$$

Jewel Bako, 79. 239 E Fifth St
☎ 979-1012. Japanese. $$-$$$$

Jing Fong, 131. 20 Elizabeth St
☎ 964-5256. Chinese. ¢-$

Joe's Shanghai, 133. 9 Pell St.
☎ 233-8888. Chinese. ¢-$$

John's Pizzeria, 31. 278 Bleecker St
☎ 243-1680. Pizza. $

Katz's Delicatessen, 90.
205 E Houston St ☎ 254-2246.
Deli. ¢-$

Kitchenette, 120. 80 W Broadway
☎ 267-6740. American. $

La Metairie, 15. 189 W 10th St
☎ 989-0343. French. $-$$

La Paella, 65. 214 E 9th St
☎ 598-4321. Spanish. $-$$

La Palapa, 61. 77 St Mark's Pl
☎ 777-2537. Mexican. $-$$

Layla, 113. 211 W Broadway
☎ 431-0700. Mediterranean. $-$$

Le Jardin, 105. 25 Cleveland Pl
☎ 343-9599. French. $-$$

Les Halles, 140. 15 John St
☎ 285-8585. French. $-$$

Le Souk, 76. 47 Avenue B
☎ 777-5454. Moroccan. $-$$

Lombardi's, 106. 32 Spring St
☎ 941-7994. Pizza. $

Lupa, 39. 170 Thompson St
☎ 982-5089. Italian. $

Macelleria, 5. 48 Gansevoort St
☎ 741-2555. Italian. $-$$$

Mary's Fish Camp, 16. 64 Charles St
☎ 646/486-2185. Seafood. $$

Megu, 129. 62 Thomas St
☎ 964-7777. Japanese. $$$

Mercer Kitchen, 53. 99 Prince St
☎ 966-5454. Contemporary. $$-$$$

Mezzogiorno, 47. 195 Spring St
☎ 334-2112. Italian. $-$$

Mingala, 71. 21-23 E 7th St
☎ 529-3656. Burmese. ¢-$$

Miracle Grill, 78. 112 First Ave
☎ 254-2353. Southwestern. $-$$

Montrachet, 111. 239 W Broadway
☎ 219-2777. French. $$-$$$

Moustache, 57. 265 E Tenth St
☎ 228-2022. Middle Eastern. ¢-$

Nam, 122. 110 Reade St
☎ 267-1777. Vietnamese. $

New Indonesia & Malaysia, 136.
18 Doyers St ☎ 267-0088.
Malaysian. ¢-$

Nobu, 115. 105 Hudson St
☎ 219-0500. Japanese. $-$$$

Nyonya, 107. 194 Grand St
☎ 334-3669. Malaysian. ¢-$

Odeon, 126. 145 W Broadway
☎ 233-0507. Bistro. $-$$

One If By Land, Two If By Sea, 23.
17 Barrow St ☎ 228-0822. Continental. $$$$

Otafuku, 66. 236 E 9th St
☎ 353-8503. Japanese. ¢

Paladar, 89. 161 Ludlow St
☎ 473-3535. Pan Latin. ¢-$

Pastis, 3. 9 Ninth Ave ☎ 929-4844.
French. $$

Pearl Oyster Bar, 27. 18 Cornelia St
☎ 691-8211. Seafood. $-$$

Petite Abeille, 32. 466 Hudson St
☎ 741-6479. Belgian. ¢-$

Pfiff, 109. 35 Grand St
☎ 334-6841. Contemporary. $-$$

Philip Marie, 18. 569 Hudson St
☎ 242-6200. New American. $

Ping's Seafood, 135. 27 Mott St
☎ 602-9988. Chinese. ¢-$$$

Pink Tea Cup, 22. 42 Grove St
☎ 807-6755. Soul. ¢-$

Pó, 26. 31 Cornelia St
☎ 645-2189. Italian. $-$$

Porcupine, 97. 20 Prince St
☎ 966-8866. American. $$

Provence, 43. 38 MacDougal St
☎ 475-7500. French. $$-$$$

Prune, 85. 54 E 1st St
☎ 677-6221. American. $-$$$

Rai Rai Ken, 69. 214 E 10th St
☎ 477-7030. Japanese. ¢

Raga, 74. 433 E 6th St
☎ 388-0957. Indian. $-$$

Raoul's, 45. 180 Prince St
☎ 966-3518. French. $$-$$$

Rialto, 91. 265 Elizabeth St
☎ 334-7900. American. ¢-$$

Rice, 104. 227 Mott St
☎ 226-5775. Eclectic. ¢-$

Roy's New York, 141.
130 Washington St ☎ 266-6262.
Pan-Asian. $$-$$$

Salaam Bombay, 119.
319 Greenwich St ☎ 226-9400.
Indian. ¢-$$

Sammy's Roumanian, 103.
157 Chrystie St ☎ 673-0330.
Eastern European. $$$

Savoy, 93. 70 Prince St
☎ 219-8570. Contemporary. $$-$$$

Second Ave Deli, 62.
156 Second Ave ☎ 677-0606.
Deli. $-$$

71 Clinton Fresh Food, 98.
71 Clinton St ☎ 614-6960.
Contemporary. $$

Snack Taverna, 33. 63 Bedford St
☎ 929-3499. Greek. $-$$

Spice Market, 2. 403 W 13th St
☎ 675-2327. Pan Asian. $-$$$

Spring Street Natural, 94.
62 Spring St ☎ 966-0290.
Healthy American. $

Strip House, 10. 13 E 12th St
☎ 328-0000. Steak. $$-$$$$

Surya, 21. 302 Bleecker St
☎ 807-7777. Indian. $-$$

Sweet 'n' Tart Restaurant, 134.
20 Mott St ☎ 964-0380. Chinese. ¢-$

Takahachi, 75. 85 Ave A
☎ 505-6524. Japanese. ¢-$$

Tasting Room, 86. 72 E 1st St
☎ 358-7831. Contemporary. ¢-$$$

Thailand, 130. 106 Bayard St
☎ 349-3132. Thai. ¢-$$

Tomoe Sushi, 40. 172 Thompson St
☎ 777-9346. Japanese. $$

Tribeca Grill, 116. 375 Greenwich St
☎ 941-3900. Contemporary. $$-$$$

2 West, 143. 2 West St (Ritz Carlton)
☎ 917/790-2525. American. $$-$$$

Veselka, 70. 144 Second Ave
☎ 228-9682. East European. ¢-$

Villa Mosconi, 38. 69 MacDougal St
☎ 673-0390. Italian. $-$$

Wallsé, 19. 344 W 11th St
☎ 352-2300. Austrian. $$-$$$

Woo Lae Oak, 51. 148 Mercer St
☎ 925-8200. Korean. $-$$

Zoë, 55. 90 Prince St
☎ 966-6722. American. $$-$$$

$$$$ = *over $35* $$$ = *$28-$35* $$ = *$19-$27* $ = *$11-$18*   ¢ = *under $10*
Based on cost per person for an entrée.

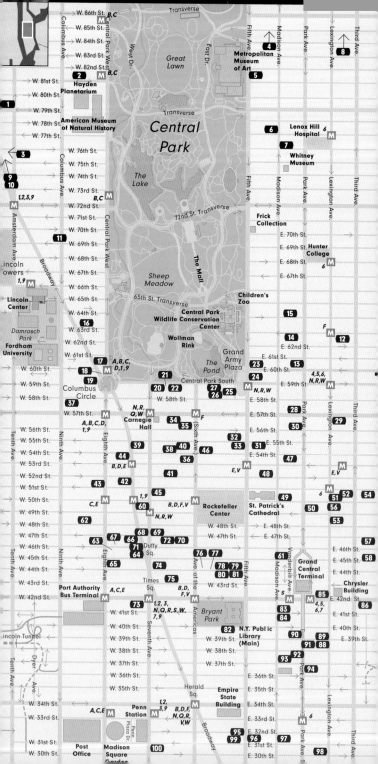

Milburn, 3. 242 W 76th St
☎ 362-1006. 📠 721-5476. $

Milford Plaza, 65. 270 W 45 St
☎ 869-3600. 📠 944-8357. ¢-$$$

Millennium Broadway, 74.
145 W 44th St ☎ 768-4400.
📠 789-7688. $-$$

Millennium Hotel UN Plaza, 59.
1 UN Plaza ☎ 758-1234. 📠 702-5051.
$$-$$$

Morgans, 93. 237 Madison Ave
☎ 686-0300. 📠 779-8352. $$

The Muse, 70. 130 W 46th St
☎ 485-2400. 📠 485-2900. $$-$$$$

NY Helmsley, 86. 212 E 42nd St
☎ 490-8900. 📠 986-4792. $-$$

NY Hilton, 36. 1335 Sixth Ave
☎ 586-7000. 📠 315-1374. $$-$$$$

NY Palace, 49. 455 Madison Ave
☎ 888-7000. 📠 303-6000. $$$$

Novotel, 42. 226 W 52nd St
☎ 315-0100. 📠 765-5365. $-$$

Omni Berkshire Place, 48. 21 E 52nd St
☎ 753-5800. 📠 754-5020. $$$

On The Ave, 10. 2177 Broadway
☎ 362-1100. 📠 787-9521. $-$$

Paramount, 67. 235 W 46th St
☎ 764-5500. 📠 354-5737. $$-$$$

The Peninsula, 33. 700 Fifth Ave
☎ 247-2200. 📠 903-3943. $$$$

Pickwick Arms, 54. 230 E 51st St
☎ 355-0300. 📠 755-5029. $

Pierre, 23. 2 E 61st St
☎ 838-8000. 📠 758-1615. $$$$

The Plaza, 25. Fifth Ave & W 59th St
☎ 759-3000. 📠 546-5324. $$$-$$$$

Plaza Athénée, 15. 37 E 64th St
☎ 734-9100. 📠 772-0958. $$$$

Plaza Fifty, 51. 155 E 50th St
☎ 751-5710. 📠 753-1468. $$-$$$

Portland Square Hotel, 72. 132 W
47th St ☎ 382-0600. 📠 382-0684. ¢-$

Ramada Inn, 98. 161 Lexington Ave
☎ 545-1800. 📠 481-7270. ¢-$

Red Roof Inn, 95. 6 W 32nd St
☎ 643-7100. 📠 643-7101. ¢-$$

Regency, 13. 540 Park Ave
☎ 759-4100. 📠 826-5674. $$$

Renaissance, 69. 714 7th Ave
☎ 765-7676. 📠 765-1962. $$$$

Rihga Royal, 38. 151 W 54th St
☎ 307-5000. 📠 765-6530. $$$-$$$$

Ritz-Carlton Central Park, 27.
50 Central Park S ☎ 308-9100.
📠 207-8831. $$$$

Roger Smith, 50. 501 Lexington
Ave ☎ 755-1400. 📠 758-4061. $-$$

Roger Williams, 97. 131 Madison Ave
☎ 448-7000. 📠 448-7007. $-$$

Roosevelt, 61. 45 E 45th St
☎ 661-9600. 📠 885-6168. $-$$$

Royalton, 80. 44 W 44th St
☎ 869-4400. 📠 575-0012. $$-$$$$

St Regis, 31. 2 E 55th St
☎ 753-4500. 📠 787-3447. $$$$

70 Park Ave, 90. 70 Park Ave
☎ 687-7050. 📠 973-2401. $$

Sheraton Russell, 94. 45 Park Ave
☎ 685-7676. 📠 889-3193. $-$$$

Sherry Netherland, 24. 781 Fifth Ave
☎ 355-2800. 📠 319-4306. $$-$$$$

Shoreham, 32. 33 W 55th St
☎ 247-6700. 📠 765-9741. $$-$$$

Sofitel New York, 78. 45 W 44th St
☎ 354-8844. 📠 782-3002. $-$$$

Southgate Tower, 100.
371 Seventh Ave ☎ 320-8050.
📠 643-8028. $$

Stanhope Park Hyatt, 5. 995 Fifth
Ave ☎ 774-1234. 📠 517-0088. $$-$$$

The Time, 61. 224 W 49th St
☎ 320-2900. 📠 245-2305. $$

**Trump International Hotel &
Towers, 18.** 1 Central Park West
☎ 299-1000. 📠 299-1150. $$$$

Vanderbilt YMCA, 57. 224 E 47th St
☎ 756-9600. 📠 752-0210. ¢-$$

W New York, 56. 541 Lexington Ave
☎ 755-1200. 📠 319-8344. $$-$$$$

W New York—The Court, 88.
130 E 39th St ☎ 685-1100.
📠 889-0287. $-$$$$

W New York—Tuscany, 89.
120 E 39th St ☎ 779-7822.
📠 696-2095. $-$$$$

W Times Square, 71. 1567 Broadway
☎ 930-7400. 📠 930-7500. $$-$$$

Waldorf–Astoria, 50. 301 Park Ave
☎ 355-3000. 📠 872-7272. $$-$$$$

Warwick, 46. 65 W 54th St
☎ 247-2700. 📠 713-1751. $$$

West Side YMCA, 16. 5 W 63rd St
☎ 875-4100. 📠 875-1334. ¢-$

Wyndham, 26. 42 W 58th St
☎ 753-3500. 📠 754-5638. $

---

*$$$$ = over $475 $$$ = $350–$475 $$ = $225–$350 $ = $110–$225   ¢ = under $110
All prices are for a standard double room, excluding 13.625% city and state sales
tax and $2 occupancy tax.*

Listed by Site Number

Best Western Seaport Inn, 35.
33 Peck Slip ☎ 766-6600.
📠 766-6615. $

Carlton Arms, 8. 160 E 25th St
☎ 684-8337. ¢

Chelsea Inn, 16. 46 W 17th St
☎ 645-8989. 📠 645-1903. ¢-$

Chelsea Lodge, 13. 318 W 20th St
☎ 243-4499. 📠 243-7852. ¢

Chelsea Savoy, 11. 204 W 23rd St
☎ 929-9353. 📠 741-6309. ¢-$$

Chelsea Star Hotel, 1. 300 W 30th St
☎ 244-7827. 📠 279-9018. $

Colonial House Inn, 12.
318 W 22nd St ☎ 633-1612. ¢-$

Cosmopolitan, 31. 95 W Broadway
☎ 566-1900. 📠 566-6909. $

Embassy Suites Hotel, 33.
102 North End Ave ☎ 945-0100.
📠 945-3012. $$-$$$$

The Gershwin, 5. 7 E 27th St
☎ 545-8000. 📠 684-5546. ¢-$$

The Giraffe, 6. 365 Park Ave S
☎ 685-7700. 📠 685-7771. $$-$$$

Gramercy Park Hotel, 17.
2 Lexington Ave ☎ 475-4320.
📠 505-0535. $-$$

Holiday Inn Downtown, 30.
138 Lafayette St ☎ 966-8898.
📠 966-3933. $-$$

Holiday Inn Wall Street, 36.
15 Gold St ☎ 232-7700. 📠 425-0330.
$-$$

Hotel Gansevoort, 15. 18 Ninth Ave
☎ 206-6700. 📠 255-5858. $$-$$$

Hotel on Rivington, 26. 107 Rivington St
☎ 475-2600. 📠 479-5959. $-$$

Hotel 17, 20. 225 E 17th St
☎ 475-2845. 📠 677-8178. ¢

Howard Johnson Express Inn, 25.
135 E Houston St ☎ 358-8844.
📠 473-3500. ¢-$

Inn at Irving Place, 18. 56 Irving Pl
☎ 533-4600. 📠 533-4611. $$-$$$$

Inn on 23rd, 10. 131 W 23rd St
☎ 463-0330. 📠 463-0302. $-$$

La Semana Hotel, 9. 25 W 24th St
☎ 255-5944. 📠 646/638-4604. $

Larchmont Hotel, 22. 27 W 11th St
☎ 989-9333. 📠 989-9496. ¢-$

Maritime Hotel, 14. 363 W 16 St
☎ 242-4300. 📠 242-1188. $$

Mercer Hotel, 27. 147 Mercer St
☎ 966-6060. 📠 965-3838. $$$-$$$$

Millennium Hilton, 34. 55 Church St
☎ 693-2001. 📠 571-2317. $$$-$$$$

NY Marriott Brooklyn, 39.
333 Adams St ☎ 718/246-7000.
📠 718/246-0563. $$

Park South Hotel, 7. 122 E 28th St
☎ 448-0888. 📠 448-0811. $-$$

Ramada Inn, 4. 161 Lexington Ave
☎ 545-1800. 📠 481-7270. $

Ritz-Carlton Battery Park, 38.
2 West St ☎ 344-0800. 📠 344-3801.
$$$-$$$$

St. Mark's Hotel, 24. 2 St Marks Pl
☎ 674-2192. 📠 420-0854. $

Second Home on Second Avenue, 21.
221 Second Ave ☎ 677-3161. $

60 Thompson, 28. 60 Thompson St
☎ 431-0400. 📠 431-0200. $$$

SoHo Grand, 29. 310 W Broadway
☎ 965-3000 📠 965-3244. $$$-$$$$

Thirty Thirty Hotel, 3. 30 E 30th St
☎ 689-1900. $

Tribeca Grand, 31. 2 Sixth Ave
☎ 519-6600. 📠 519-6700. $$-$$$

W-Union Square, 19. 201 Park Ave S
☎ 253-9119. 📠 779-0148. $$-$$$

Wall Street Inn, 37. 9 William St
☎ 747-1500. 📠 747-1900. $$

Washington Square Hotel, 23.
103 Waverly Pl ☎ 777-9515.
📠 979-8373. $

Wolcott Hotel, 2. 3 W 31st St
☎ 268-2900. ¢

$$$$ = over $475 $$$ = $350-$475 $$ = $225-$350 $ = $110-$225   ¢ = under $110
*All prices are for a standard double room, excluding 13.625% city and state sales
tax and $2 occupancy tax.*

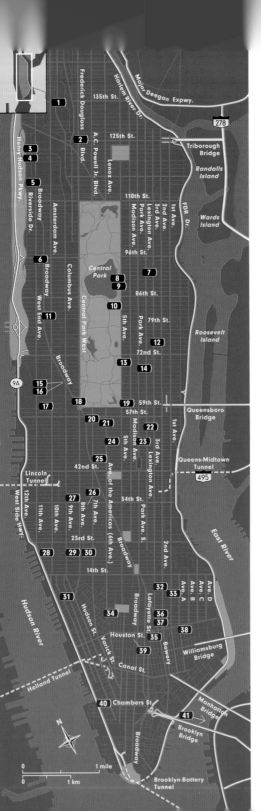

Listed Alphabetically

Aaron Davis Hall, 1.
135 Convent Ave ☎ 650–7100

Amato Opera, 37.
319 Bowery ☎ 228–8200

Angel Orensanz Foundation, 38.
172 Norfolk St ☎ 529–7194

Apollo Theater, 2.
253 W 125th St ☎ 749–5838

Beacon Theater, 11.
2124 Broadway ☎ 496–7070

Brooklyn Academy of Music, 41.
30 Lafayette Ave ☎ 718/636–4100

Carnegie Hall, 20.
154 W 57th St ☎ 247–7800

Church of the Heavenly Rest, 8.
2 E 90th St ☎ 289–3400

City Center, 21.
131 W 55th St ☎ 581–1212

Cunningham Studio, 31.
55 Bethune St ☎ 691–9751

Dance Theatre Workshop, 30.
219 W 19th St ☎ 924–0077

DiCapo Opera Theater, 12.
184 E 76th St ☎ 288–9438

Dixon Place, 35.
258 Bowery ☎ 219–0736

Florence Gould Hall, 19.
55 E 59th St ☎ 355–6160

Frick Museum, 13.
1 E 70th St ☎ 288–0700

Guggenheim Museum, 9.
1071 Fifth Ave ☎ 423–3500

Hammerstein Ballroom, 27.
311 W 34th St ☎ 307–7171

Jazz at Lincoln Center, 18.
Broadway & 60th St ☎ 258–9800

John Jay Theater, 17.
899 Tenth Ave ☎ 237–8000

Joyce SoHo, 38.
155 Mercer St ☎ 334–7479

Joyce Theater, 29.
175 Eighth Ave ☎ 242–0800

Kaye Playhouse, 14.
695 Park Ave ☎ 772–4448

The Kitchen, 28.
512 W 19th St ☎ 255–5793

La MaMa ETC, 36.
74A E 4th St ☎ 475–7710

Lincoln Center, 16.
Broadway & 64th St
☎ 875–5000
·Alice Tully Hall ☎ 721–6500
·Avery Fisher Hall☎ 875–5030
·Juilliard Theatre ☎ 769–7406
·Metropolitan Opera ☎ 362–6000
·Mitzi E Newhouse Theater
☎ 239–6200
·NY State Theater ☎ 870–5570
·Vivian Beaumont Theater
☎ 239–6200

Madison Square Garden, 26.
Seventh Ave & 32nd St ☎ 465–6741

Manhattan School of Music, 3.
120 Claremont Ave ☎ 749–2802

Merkin Concert Hall, 17.
129 W 67th St ☎ 501–3330

Metropolitan Museum, 10.
1000 Fifth Ave ☎ 570–3949

Miller Theater, 5. Columbia Univ,
Broadway & W 116th St ☎ 854–7799

92nd St Y, 7.
1395 Lexington Ave ☎ 415–5500

PS 122, 33.
150 First Ave ☎ 477–5288

Radio City Music Hall, 24.
1260 Sixth Ave ☎ 247–4777

Riverside Church, 4.
120th St & Riverside Dr ☎ 870–6784

St Bartholomew's Church, 23.
109 E 50th St ☎ 378–0200

St Mark's-in-the-Bowery, 32.
Second Ave & 10th St ☎ 674–8194

St Peter's Church, 22.
619 Lexington Ave ☎ 935–2200

Symphony Space, 6.
2537 Broadway ☎ 864–5400

Town Hall, 25.
123 W 43rd St ☎ 840–2824

**TriBeCa Performing Arts
Center, 39.** 199 Chambers St
☎ 220–1460

Washington Square Church, 34.
135 W 4th St ☎ 777–2528

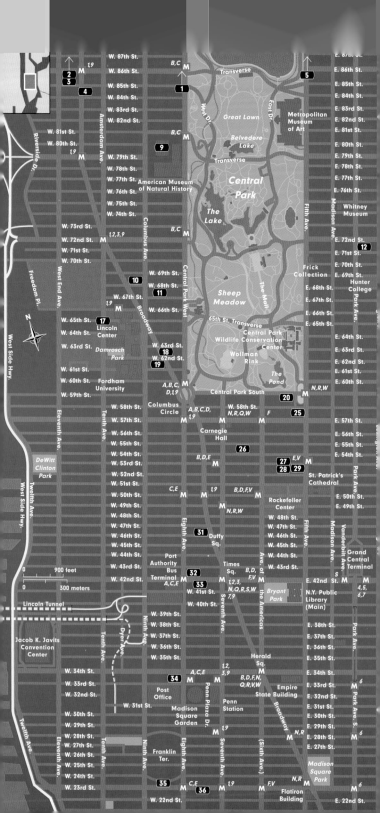

Listed by Site Number

AMC Empire 25, 33.
234 W 42nd St ☎ 398-3939

Asia Society, 12.
725 Park Ave ☎ 288-6400

City Cinemas 1, 2, 3, 21.
Third Ave & 60th St ☎ 777-FILM #635

City Cinemas East 86th St, 7.
210 E 86th St ☎ 734-4427

City Cinemas Sutton I & 2, 24.
Third Ave & 57th St ☎ 759-1412

Clearview's Beekman, 15.
1254 Second Ave ☎ 737-2622

Clearview's Chelsea (1–9), 36.
260 W 23rd St ☎ 777-FILM #597

Clearview's Chelsea West, 35.
333 W 23rd St ☎ 989-0061

Clearview's 59th St East Cinema, 23.
239 E 59th St ☎ 777-FILM #615

**Clearview's First & 62nd Cinemas
(1–6), 22.** 400 E 62nd St ☎ 513-5408

Clearview's Metro Twin, 2.
Broadway & 99th St ☎ 777-FILM #609

Clearview's 62nd & Broadway, 19.
Broadway & 62nd St ☎ 777-FILM #864

Clearview's Ziegfeld Theatre, 26.
141 W 54th St ☎ 765-7600

Crown NY Twin, 14.
1271 Second Ave ☎ 249-4200

Donnell Library Media Center, 28.
20 W 53rd St ☎ 621-0618

French Institute, 20.
55 E 59th St ☎ 355-6100

Guggenheim Museum, 5.
1071 Fifth Ave ☎ 423-3500

Japan Society, 30.
333 E 47th St ☎ 832-1155

Lincoln Plaza Cinemas (1-6), 18.
B'way & 63rd St ☎ 757-2280

Loews 84th St, 4.
2310 Broadway ☎ 50L-OEWS #701

Loews Cineplex E Walk, 32.
8th Ave & 42nd St ☎ 50L-OEWS #572

Loews Kips Bay, 37.
570 Second Ave ☎ 50L-OEWS #558

Loews Lincoln Square (1-13), 10.
1998 Broadway ☎ 336-5000

Loews Orpheum VIII, 6.
1538 Third Ave
☎ 800/FANDANGO #778

Loews 72nd St East, 13.
1230 Third Ave ☎ 879-1313

Loews State, 31.
Broadway & 46th St ☎ 50L-OEWS

Loews 34th St, 34.
312 W 34th St ☎ 244-8850

Magic Johnson's Harlem USA, 1.
124th St & Frederick Douglass Blvd
☎ 665-8742

Makor, 11. 35 W 67th St ☎ 601-1000

Museum of Television and Radio, 29.
25 W 52nd St ☎ 621-6800

Naturemax, 9.
American Museum of Natural History,
Central Park W & 79th St ☎ 769-5100

Paris, 25. 4 W 58th St ☎ 688-3800

Symphony Space, 3.
Broadway & 95th St ☎ 864-5400

United Artist East, 8.
First Ave & 85th St ☎ 249-5100

United Artist Gemini, 16.
Second Ave & 64th St
☎ 800/FANDANGO #626

Walter Reade Theater, 17.
165 W 65th St ☎ 875-5600

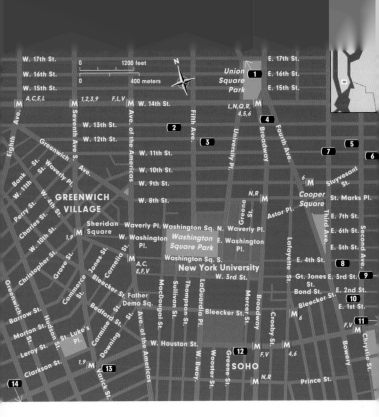

Hudson River

Riverside Park

Riverside Drive

Broadway

W. 113th St.
W. 112th St.
W. 111th St.
M W. 110th St.
1,9
W. 109th St.
W. 108th St.
W. 107th St.
W. 106th St.
W. 105th St.
W. 104th St.
1,9
W. 103rd St. M
W. 102nd St.
W. 101st St.
W. 100th St.
W. 99th St.
W. 98th St.

Cathedral of St. John the Divine
Cathedral Parkway
Duke Ellington Blvd.

Amsterdam Ave.
Columbus Ave.
Manhattan Ave.

Frederick Douglass Circle
Central Park N. M
St. Nicholas Ave.
Lenox Ave.
Fifth Ave.
2,3

Central Park West

Harlem Meer
El Museo del Barrio
Museum of the City of NY

The Loch
The Pool
North Meadow
East Meadow
Transverse

Straus Park
3

M
1,2,3,9
W. 97th St.
W. 96th St.
W. 95th St.
W. 94th St.
W. 93rd St.
W. 92nd St.
W. 91st St.
W. 90th St.
W. 89th St.
W. 88th St.
W. 87th St.
W. 86th St.
W. 85th St.
W. 84th St.
W. 83rd St.
W. 82nd St.
W. 81st St.
W. 80th St.
W. 79th St.
W. 78th St.
W. 77th St.
W. 76th St.
W. 75th St.
W. 74th St.
W. 73rd St.
W. 72nd St.
W. 71st St.
W. 70th St.
W. 69th St.
W. 68th St.
W. 67th St.
W. 66th St.
W. 65th St.
W. 64th St.
W. 63rd St.
W. 61st St.
W. 60th St.
W. 59th St.
W. 58th St.
W. 57th St.
W. 56th St.
W. 55th St.
W. 54th St.
W. 53rd St.
W. 52nd St.
W. 51st St.
W. 50th St.
W. 49th St.

B,C

West End Ave.
Broadway

Joan of Arc Park
4

Jewish Museum
Cooper-Hewitt Museum
National Academy of Design
Guggenheim Museum

The Reservoir

Transverse

5
6

CENTRAL PARK
Great Lawn

West Dr.
East Dr.

Belvedere Lake
Transverse

Hayden Planetarium
8
9
10
11
12
14

American Museum of Natural History

The Lake

Metropolitan Museum of Art

15 16

1,2,3,9 M

Fifth Ave.

B,C

17
18

M
1,9

Sheep Meadow
Transverse

Frick Collection

The Mall

Lincoln Center

Damrosch Park

Fordham University

Freedom Pl.
West End Ave.

Central Park Wildlife Conservation Center
Wollman Rink

The Pond

27

Grand Army Plaza
N,R,W

26

Central Park South

A,B,C, D,1,9 M
29
30

Columbus Circle
28

N,R,Q,W

F

Tenth Ave.
Ninth Ave.
Eighth Ave.
Seventh Ave.
Ave. of the Americas
Fifth Ave.

A,B,C,D, 1,9

Carnegie Hall
32
33
34

B,D,E

E,V

36
37
38

C,E
N,R,W

1,9 M

Rockefeller Center
B,D,F,V

0   900 feet
0 300 meters

N

Eleventh Ave.
Twelfth Ave.
West Side Hwy.

31

DeWitt Clinton Park

1
2

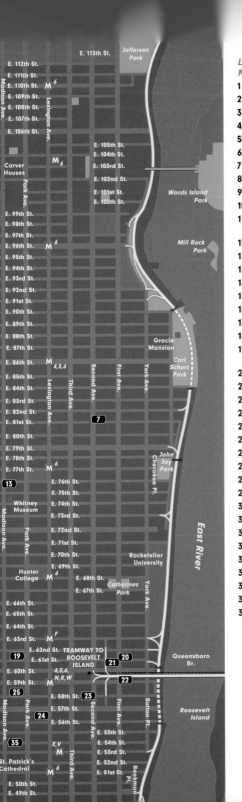